HOW TO SUCCEED IN THE BEAUTY BUSINESS

CIARA ALLEN

An Orange Publishing Book

How To Succeed in the Beauty Business by Ciara Allen

First published in Ireland in 2017 as a paperback original
by Orange Publishing

Typeset, illustrations and cover design by Conor Merriman
Printed and bound by Print Bureau, 23 Goldenbridge Ind. Est. Dublin 8
www.printbureau.ie

First Printing, 2017
ISBN 978-1- 5272-1313- 5

www.ciaraallen.net

For Dolores, who made me feel like I finally understood where my creativity and love of coffee came from.

For Paul, who never stopped believing in me, even when I'd stopped believing in myself. I owe you everything.

CONTENTS

INTRODUCTION

Believe it or not, this book originally started off as a blog post. I thought writing books was for people who went to college for 17 years, studying a subject so unusual that it takes more than ten minutes to explain. For those who understood politics in more depth than my categories (the 'good' and the 'not so good' ones) when rating politicians for an upcoming election. But a book was written, and, sure, here it is.

I put out a call on my social media accounts in early 2017 to see if any makeup artists had any questions that I could answer. As someone who struggled to find her feet in the industry, I understand more than anyone how challenging and lonely it can be; isolating, even. Sometimes you don't know what direction to turn, and most of the time you don't even know where to start. Of course, you can do a makeup course – but what happens afterwards? Who's going to help you then? What if your sights are set past a glossy makeup counter, onto a photoshoot for Vogue Magazine? Who teaches you how to get there? I've realised that there are so many things you have to learn as you go – but luckily for you, I've put every ounce of my industry knowledge into this book. You're welcome!

I was expecting a handful of responses to my call for questions, but ended up with a lot more than I could answer in a simple blog post. You see, I got more than a hundred responses. Among them, there was a general feeling of confusion around certain industry topics, and I understood what was behind each question. I knew how every artist felt as they carefully wrote their question under my post, avoiding typos wherever possible and ending it with a cute emoji. Armed with all of these questions, I sat down and began writing. There was no quick one-word answer, so after about an hour I had only finished number four and realised that a blog just wouldn't be enough, a book was the only option.

Doing what you love isn't necessarily the easiest option – but I guess, deep down, we all know that already. In most cases, you usually have to choose between the career you don't want but will make you a lot of money or the job of your dreams that will enrich your life, but that pays very little. Unfortunately, we all can't follow our dreams because of financial commitments like mortgages, kids, etc. If it weren't for the support, love and constant encouragement of my husband Paul, I would have given up a long time ago. There is absolutely no doubt in my mind about that. When I was suffering from low confidence, he would always help to build me back up, and he still does to this day. When people wouldn't respond to my emails or phone calls, he'd remind me that everything would work out just the way it was supposed to. And you know what? He was right. It can still be hard sometimes, as freelance work, though exciting, is unpredictable, last-minute cancellations are frequent and invoices can need a lot of chasing to get paid. With all of that said, I would never change what I do. I feel so lucky to have a job that I love, and I don't take anything for granted. I've learned to be strong, to be confident in my craft and to fight for every job that I get.

This book focuses on the advice I wish I'd been given at the beginning. It's so easy to forget, but we're all in this together, we all have similar hopes and dreams, and it's not a race to the end. There are no winners or losers, just those who try and those who don't.

So be a trier – they're my personal favourite.

STAGE 1:

GETTING STARTED

Sometimes the hardest thing to do is figuring out where to start. After that – sure, you're flying!

1.1 MAKEUP COURSES

Finding your feet in any creative field can be difficult, to say the least. Some of the most naturally talented people will have never studied, while others can train for years and still struggle to create. I always say that being a makeup artist is 50 percent the makeup you do and 50 percent how you are with people. You could be the world's most talented artist, but if you're difficult to work with and find it hard to get along with others, you will struggle.

It's a controversial point, but I don't think expensive makeup courses are always the best option for getting into the industry. Some of the world's most famous makeup artists are self-taught, so keep that in mind. Ireland, after all, is a tiny country. It's different in places like Paris and London where they are spoiled with a variety of courses and colleges; their tutors are professionals who collectively hold decades of experience in the industry. Unfortunately, some of the makeup schools in Ireland take a dark road when it comes to hiring their tutors: for example, a student, with no prior experience, might complete a two-month course only to be hired by the school to teach the next one. It sounds ludicrous, but it's true. This student will be built up with false promises and manipulated for the advantage of the company. Having spent only a few weeks getting to grips with the basics themselves, at this stage of their learning they desperately need constant guidance and tuition. The artist in no way benefits from this situation and, to top it all off, they will be paid very little.

This set-up, over time, will lead to incorrect information and bad habits being passed on to new fee-paying students, unnoticed. The part-time course that I did back at the beginning was also not all that it seemed. It could be summed up as disorganised and over-priced, with no decent product being used in class. The school was 'all fluff': all image and no substance. So trust me: I have first-hand experience of being €3,000 out of pocket on course fees, with nothing to show for it except a crude 'degree' certificate that wasn't worth the paper it was printed on.

If you're looking into doing a makeup course, I recommend you do the following:

Find out who's on the faculty

Do your research and find out who the tutors are. A course is only as good as the person teaching it, so keep your standards high and don't compromise. Also, consider the following:

- Is the tutor actually working in the industry? If so, for how long?
- In what area do they work? Do they specialise in fashion and beauty? Are they a special-effects artist? Have they only ever worked on a makeup counter?
- Are there reviews of them online? Have they had satisfied students/clients in the past?
- How impressive is their website? Do you like their portfolio? Is it inspiring? Is it the standard you would expect a tutor's work to be? (Note: If they don't have a website, I would be concerned.)
- Who have they worked with? Do they work on commercials for large companies? Has their work been published in magazines?
- Do they have TV and Film experience? If so, with whom?
- How do they come across on social media? Do they seem friendly, confident and hardworking, or like someone who's difficult to get along with?

Go and see for yourself

Before you hand over any money, go and visit the school to make sure that they're everything that they advertise. Be wary of a company that won't let you visit the building before you enrol. When you walk into the building, excitement can easily take over, but remember to keep your eyes and ears peeled at all times for any signs that something isn't quite right. By going at peak times, you'll see how the school functions with a high volume of students, as well as the facilities that are available. Also, see what kind of feeling you get from their current students: are they happy? Are they glad they chose this course? Do they have any regrets?

Do your research

Unfortunately, companies can now instantly buy large online followings, so even if a school has 50,000+ followers, don't take it for granted that they're legitimate and can be trusted. Bad reviews can easily be deleted, and in some cases, schools can even issue the reviewer with a solicitor's letter to demand the post's instant removal. Have a good look through your prospective school's social media history and read about their students' experiences. If a school has recently removed their review section, there's a reason why – and trust me, it's not a good one.

Consider part-time study

A full-time course is a huge commitment, particularly if you need to keep working, so why not try part-time first and see how you get on. Then, if it's the right path for you and you've found the perfect school, go for it!

Check the products they use

Be suspicious of a school that has only their 'own brand' available for use in the classroom. Unless they're a world-renowned beauty school with a huge budget for product development and lab testing, they've most likely bought in generic, low-grade products and stamped their name on the packaging. They didn't create these products, they haven't had any input into their development, and if you buy them, you'll most likely be paying at least ten times what the school bought them for. Having a diverse product knowledge is essential, and you need experience working with a range of brands from the beginning.

The same goes for brushes. If a school tries to sell you their own brand of brushes, ask where they get them manufactured and who designed them. The majority of brushes come from China, and a lot of companies buy generic brushes in bulk, stamp their name on the handle and joyously claim that they are their own. There's nothing wrong with brushes from China – the majority of them are made there – but what does matter is that you fully understand what you're buying. For the same price, you could buy brushes from a reputable brand, knowing that there's little-to-no risk of them falling apart.

Don't rush

If the school is pressuring you into making a decision, I would always say, 'Follow your gut instinct'. If you feel that something isn't quite right, don't ignore it.

1.2 BOOKS & SOCIAL MEDIA

There's a lot to be said for being a self-taught makeup artist, as we now have constant access to a wealth of information via the Internet. Back when I was starting out, there was no such thing as social media, no mobile data or smartphones. Things are much easier now with information only ever being a click or a swipe away. Starting out I found inspiration in Fashion Magazines and makeup books and still do after all of these years.

Books

Even though trends are temporary and fads are fleeting, some makeup books will be cherished forever. Below are some of my personal favourites:

Kevyn Aucoin

Born in 1962, Kevyn was one of America's most famous and cherished makeup artists. Working with the likes of Tina Turner, Madonna, Naomi Campbell and Cindy Crawford, his work has been published all over the world in Vogue, Cosmopolitan and any other fashion magazine worth reading. His beauty ideal focused on showing women the natural beauty they possess and how to enhance instead of hiding it. His work was simplistic but expertly applied. Sadly, he passed away in 2002, but his philosophy still lives on in his books Making Faces, Face Forward and The Art of Makeup.

Rae Morris

Rae is a fantastic Australian makeup artist who penned one of my favourite books, aptly called Makeup: The Ultimate Guide. The book delivers a variety of colourful, simple and fresh beauty looks and her use of metallics and loose pigments is breathtaking.

Alex Box

One of the world's most creative visionaries, Alex possesses a style that is both unique and bold whilst always being beautiful. Her background in fine art is evident in her conceptual work and through every brush stroke, final dusting of pigment and bold blend of colour. I've looked up to Alex for many years, and it's unsurprising that she's worked with the likes of

Alexander McQueen, Lady Gaga, Vivienne Westwood and Chanel to name only a handful. Her book, Alex Box by Rankin, though difficult to find these days, is as beautiful as it is inspirational. When I first started out and opted for more colourful and artistic styles of makeup, she made me feel like I wasn't alone in this idea.

Social media

Youtube

It's hard to believe that the first video ever uploaded to Youtube was only back on April 23rd, 2005. It was a short, 19-second clip of a guy at the zoo talking about elephants. Only 12 years later, 3.25 billion hours of video are watched monthly, all over the world. Youtube gave makeup a platform, as normal people, just like you and I, could share our daily routines, favourite products and join a community of like-minded people. It's a free service, so anyone can log on and upload. Makeup tutorials now make up (get it?) a huge portion of the most watched videos online, and it's quickly become an industry all of its own.

I used to follow a lot of beauty channels, but over time, I've slowly started to click the unsubscribe button. It's hard to find someone that can still be interesting even after a few hundred videos. For me, Lisa Eldridge has always been my favourite. She's a renowned London-based makeup artist who has worked with the likes of Kate Winslet, Cara Delevingne and Kate Moss, as well as having her work published in Vogue, Love magazine and Harper's Bazaar. Her videos are a fantastic source of inspiration for beautiful makeup looks, as well as having a wealth of invaluable information for makeup artists.

Instagram

It's a vital tool for all businesses, but is particularly essential for those in the fashion industry: it's never been easier for you to contact well-known figures in the industry. Back in pre-Internet days, you would've had to physically post your portfolio book to be seen by a magazine editor or an agent and then patiently wait for its return. Now you can tag them in your post and hope that they see it. The legendary makeup artist Pat McGrath is great at supporting new and upcoming artists by 'liking' their work, as well as leaving them the occasional comment. Now, it's not to say that she'll call you up the next day and invite you to work alongside her at Fashion Week, but hey, you never know. Pat (yes, we're on first-name terms, what of it?) follows me on Instagram and once or twice a month I double check to make sure that she hasn't, for whatever reason, unfollowed me. It's inevitable that it will happen one day but I don't know if I could take that kind of heartbreak. Cue heavy rain, dramatic arm movements and Celine Dion ballads.

Don't underestimate how powerful Instagram can be in helping you market your work to a larger audience. It's a great way to see what goes on behind the scenes on shoots for top magazines and to see what products your favourite artists like to use on set. Some of my personal favourite accounts to follow at the moment are @thevalgarland, @patmcgrathreal, @andrewgallimakeup, @thealexbox, @isamayaffrench and @lisaeldridgemakeup.

1.3 BECOMING AN ASSISTANT

Being an assistant to an already established makeup artist is, in a way, a rite of passage in the industry. So much can be learnt when you get the opportunity to see how another artist works – things that you could never learn in a classroom. Assisting will show you how a photoshoot runs, who does what job on set and the amount of time it can take to get a shot just right. This can sometimes take hours, so make sure you always wear comfy shoes.

Assisting generally tends to be unpaid, unless you build up a good working relationship with the artist you're working with over time. In some situations, they may want to hire you on a full-time basis, which is a fantastic opportunity. It's important to understand that by taking you on as an assistant, the artist is going to be investing their time in you and it's important not to take that for granted. So many people would love the opportunity to see what goes on behind the scenes, so don't ever get too comfortable – assistants are easy to replace.

Your job, when assisting, is to make the artist's day as easy as possible and not to be out for yourself while on set. For example, handing out your business cards to the crew while assisting is a big mistake. It's disrespectful to the artist and can make them look bad. If, for instance, someone on set asks for your contact details, put it past the artist before you do anything. They will not only appreciate your honesty but will also tell you if it's OK or not.

How do you become an assistant?

It's important, as a new artist, to educate yourself on the industry and to identify what area you want to work in. If you choose fashion, for example, do some research by flicking through the latest issues of magazines and making a list of the artists credited at the end of the shoots. Once you have a list, find their email addresses, write a well-phrased email and hit send. Here's an example of what I'd write:

> *To [name],*
>
> *I hope you are keeping well.*
> *I wanted to send you an email to introduce myself.*
> *My name is [your name] and I'm a newly qualified makeup artist in the industry. I'm a really big fan of your work, particularly your recent work in [fashion magazine].*
> *I have attached some pictures of my work, as well as my CV.*
>
> *I was wondering if you ever need an assistant? I would love the opportunity to work with you, should you ever need some help.*
>
> *My contact details are below should you need them:*
> *Email: [your email address]*
> *Phone: [your phone number]*
>
> *Kindest Regards,*
> *[Your name]*

Some people mightn't necessarily reply to your email, but if you really like their work, I'd recommend following up with them on a fortnightly/monthly basis until you get a reply. Better to get a reply saying 'no' than to get no response at all. Do be aware that the artists you're contacting are under no obligation to respond – but I would hope they do, as we all started off somewhere. When following up with them, keep in mind that they might be very busy with work and family, so be patient. Each time you write, always be friendly and polite and, even if you're angry with them, never let it be known or felt in your email. You don't want to give them an excuse not to reply, so always be nice.

What does being an assistant entail?

Going with the artist on jobs, to learn, observe and assist if needed

You mightn't get to do any makeup, but that isn't the point of being there. You need to be alert and ready for whatever tasks the artist might need you for. If they need you to run to a makeup store to get something, your job is to happily oblige.

Helping the crew in any way you can

On a long shoot, doing a coffee run or picking up lunch for everyone is a huge help, as is being on hand for any small jobs that need doing. When I was assisting, the list could include getting cigarettes for the model, running to pick up some clothes for the stylist or moving the Photographers car. Always be happy to help and you'll be a pleasure to have on set instead of a burden.

Prepping, cleaning and organising the artist's kit and brushes if requested

Take on as many of the menial jobs as possible to make the artist's life a bit easier. Do check with the artist, though, before you start rearranging things, as they most likely have their own way they like to organise their kit. Again, remember: you're there to make their life easier, not more challenging.

Setting up the artist's station if requested and keeping it tidy throughout the day

If you're working with an artist for the first time, don't presume that they set up their station the same way you do. Everyone has their own way of doing things, so just be on hand to help should they need you. The least you can do is get rid of any used wipes, cotton buds and mascara wands – do always check with the artist first. Over time as you learn how they work, you can help out more in this area, but at the beginning just watch and learn.

Keeping your ego at bay

Regardless of what jobs or experience you've previously had, you're there to help in any way you can, so don't act like some tasks are beneath you. If your ego gets in the way, you're in for a rude awakening. As Drake said so eloquently, 'Started from the bottom …' You can't just start out and suddenly get booked to work on shoots for Italian Vogue or work with A-list stars. If you're only assisting on this one job, enjoy every second of it and stay on your toes.

Always being early

Punctuality shows professionalism and that you care, so always be at least 10–15 minutes early. You can then help the crew unload any equipment into the studio and without really trying, you're already making a good impression. Introduce yourself as the makeup artist's assistant. If they haven't arrived yet, shake hands and be friendly to every member of the crew, no exceptions.

Making mistakes on set

Unfortunately, this will happen and while you need to learn from your mistakes, don't let them destroy you. Back when I was assisting, I made a mistake on set and got so upset over it. What happened? I was on a photoshoot with an artist and a photographer, both of whom I really admired. They were shooting beauty looks, and I was having the most amazing time. As they worked, I took a picture of the monitor, showing the raw image directly from the photographer's camera, unedited, and uploaded it on to my Facebook page. The artist I was assisting called me the next day to say that the photographer was furious, and that I needed

to take the image down immediately and email him to apologise.
I couldn't believe it – I'd messed up and it was all over.

I quickly logged on to my account, deleted the post and started
to write an apologetic email to the photographer. I was very polite,
mentioned who I was in case he didn't know me by name and apologised
profusely. I explained that as a new artist to the industry, I was still
learning how things worked and that I was very sorry. I told him that I
learned a valuable lesson that I would always remember. He responded,
saying that it was fine and thanked me.

Mistakes are unfortunately inevitable, but the important thing is that
you don't keep making the same ones over and over. Artists will usually
forgive you once, but after that, they may stop calling you altogether.
I learned a valuable lesson that day about being careful of what I post
on social media while on set. If you're assisting, always ask the artist
if it's OK to post something. If it's your own job, ask the client or
photographer.

Dressing appropriately

It's important to make sure that you present yourself professionally, but
make sure you're appropriately dressed for the type of job you're going
on. If the shoot is outdoors and up in the mountains, wear something
comfortable, warm and, most importantly, wear suitable shoes. Don't
wear high heels unless the artist requests you do so. Dress codes also vary
depending on the type of work you do; for example, film is very casual
while a commercial for a bank will be more formal. If in doubt, ask the
artist what they'd like you to wear. Remember you are there representing
them, not just yourself.

Staying out of the way

By getting in the crew's way, you'll end up being a burden instead of another helpful pair of hands. Of course, you'll want to see what's going on, but you need to understand your place; so stay back and fade into the background until you're needed.

Bringing your own food

Most of the time on photoshoots, the client will order lunch for the entire crew, but sometimes, due to restricted budgets, there mightn't be much food to go around. Bring along your own lunch and a bottle of water so you're not adding any extra expense to the shoot.

Doing your research on the crew

The artist you're assisting mightn't necessarily share the team's details with you, but if they do, research the photographer, stylist and model. You never know who you might be getting the chance to meet.

Never missing an opportunity because you have plans

I couldn't tell you how many events, movie dates and concerts I've had to miss because a job came up at the last minute. It sounds cruel, but sometimes you only get one chance, so unless you have surgery scheduled, take the job. (I actually did reschedule surgery back in 2016 so I could do a magazine shoot – but more on that later.)

Remembering the big picture

When you're an established makeup artist and take on an assistant yourself, you'll quickly learn that if you can't trust them to be around your clients, you simply can't bring them on set. They will be a detriment to have around, and that defeats the purpose. So, with that in mind, you need to be polite, friendly, punctual and not on your phone all day.

Be careful what you say in front of the crew or the client and don't comment on what's being photographed. You are there to observe, not provide art direction. Stay close to the artist you're assisting and if you have any questions, go directly to them, not to any other member of the crew.

Things you shouldn't do while assisting

- Be out for yourself.
- Show up hungover.
- Smoke.
- Get involved in any drama on set.
- Give your opinion on the shoot.
- Get in the crew's way.
- Be rude.
- Use your phone all the time.
- Talk excessively.
- Talk badly about people.
- Be rude to the models.

Don't stay an assistant forever

I assisted a makeup artist for about two years before going it alone. While I did learn a lot in this time, I felt that I no longer wanted to be associated with any other artist except myself. It was a scary decision, but I'm so glad I did it.

STAGE 2:

BUILDING YOUR BRAND

Because if you don't hustle for work as a freelancer, the only phone calls you'll be getting will be from debt collectors ...

2.1 INDUSTRY TERMS & ADVICE

Below is a list of the main industry terminology you'll hear and need
to understand.

Advertising agency
A company hired by a brand to come up with the concept as well as
the execution of an ad campaign. They also usually hire the crew for
the shoot.

Advertorial
This is like a Fashion Editorial, but it's sponsored by a brand or company.
The looks will focus around the style of the brand and the company pays
the entire team, including hair and makeup. Advertorials should never
be unpaid.

Agent
An agent is a person who acts on behalf of another person. If you are
represented by an agent, they will help to get you booked for work in
return for taking a commission of around 20 per cent. Agents represent
models, actors, photographers, stylists, makeup artists, hairstylists, etc.

Beauty editor
You guessed it – the person responsible for overall beauty content in a
magazine.

Beauty shoot
Anything based around the term 'beauty' has a focus on the face. Think
of a makeup campaign promoting a new foundation: there may be

elements of styling, but the makeup and model are the key features.

Brief

Before a shoot, you will usually be given a 'brief', or set of instructions, outlining the look that the client wants you to create. This can be verbal or in the form of a moodboard, which I mention again on page 42. Again, be sure to stick to your brief and give your opinion and thoughts if asked. Sometimes the client will want you to come up with the makeup look yourself, while other times they will have something very specific in mind that they will want you to create.

Callsheet

This is a document sent out to the entire crew before a shoot, detailing the schedule, location, contact details, and other essential information.

Commercial

A commercial shoot is one based around a company, usually in the form of an advertisement or – you guessed it – a commercial. These are generally simple in terms of the makeup needed as they are often based on recreating real-life scenarios (not always though). Commercial clients can be companies like supermarkets, banks and retailers.

Concept

This term refers to the idea or theme of a shoot. Usually put together by the photographer or stylist, the concept, once finalised, will be shared with the rest of the team. It's very important that you stick to the look you've been asked to create so the entire shoot will be cohesive. If it's a bridal shoot and you decide to do a wild black glossy eye with diamanté lashes, you have totally veered off concept and risk ruining the entire shoot.

Credit

This is what a magazine will print on the final page of the shoot, it will read: Makeup by Ciara Allen, using [product].

Director/Art director/Creative director

This is the person with overall responsibility for the entire production or photoshoot. With this responsibility comes a great deal of pressure as they are setting the tone and style for the project.

Fashion editorial

This is a photoshoot for a magazine that will usually have eight to ten looks. They can vary widely, with themes and can be both wildly dramatic as well as soft and subtle.

Lighting technician

In charge of the light equipment on set as well as its maintenance and the safety of the team around the equipment.

Magazine editor

Person responsible for the overall content in a magazine or an online publication.

Model

The person showing the pieces on a shoot. The type of model can vary hugely, depending on what the shoot is for. For fashion shoots, some models can be rather unusual looking, but this is what makes them special. For a commercial shoot, say for a sportswear company, they would book a model who represents their brand and customer base. Models come in all shapes and sizes so please understand that they are people too: they need to be looked after on set and as makeup artists we have a responsibility to them, as we work so closely together. They can be as young as fourteen or as old as one hundred, so be respectful, be kind and never speak about them as if they aren't there.

Moodboard

Usually in a PDF format, a moodboard will communicate the concept of a shoot using images. These are often put together by a stylist or a photographer, and will include styling references as well as some hair and makeup ones.

Photographer

You guessed it, the person with the camera, who takes the pictures. Most people still expect them to always be male but I know some really awesome female photographers so never presume.

Producer

The producer is responsible for the management of a project as well as its finances.

Samples

Sometimes the clothes will be borrowed directly from shops, or they might be samples that are sent directly from the clothing brand. Samples can be from an upcoming collection that hasn't yet been released. The stylist will usually be more relaxed working with samples because if they get dirty on a photoshoot, they are not required to pay for them as they don't need to be returned for resale to a shop.

Set designer/Art department

This is the individual or team responsible for the overall look of either a film or a photoshoot. This includes building a set with props and furniture if necessary – and no, this is not as easy as it sounds.

Stylist

The person in charge of the clothes/wardrobe. The stylist and photographer work closely to come up with a concept for the shoot. Be very careful around the clothes on set as the garments can be worth a lot of money and are the sole responsibility of the stylist. If they're not returned in perfect condition after the shoot, the stylist will have to pay for the item.

Test shoot

This is when creatives come together to do a photoshoot for their portfolio. No one receives any payment as this is an opportunity for everyone to be creative. This could be just a photographer, model and a makeup artist or a full team, which could also include a stylist and a hairstylist. This will help you to build up your portfolio and make contacts, but note that these images cannot be used to generate any direct income without the entire team's permission. For example, if you were placing an ad in a magazine with one of the images created on a test shoot, you would need to get the permission of the entire team first.

General advice

To keep things simple, below are some key points that I strongly urge you to pay close attention to:

Never put anything in writing that you wouldn't want to be quoted on

This goes for emails, texts and interactions on all forms of social media, whether you're using your personal or business accounts.

Don't get drunk with the people you work with

This blurs the boundaries of work and play and can get you into a great deal of trouble. If you want to be taken seriously in what you do, remember that you're representing your business 24/7 – don't compromise that for a few pints.

Never bad mouth a colleague

You don't want to be labelled as someone who gossips at work, and I've learned that it's always better to stay quiet and not get involved when it comes to any drama on set. At the end of the day, they're just people you work with and it really doesn't matter if you like them or not.

Always be at least ten minutes early

No exceptions. If I can, I arrive an hour early, get a coffee and then get set up before the rest of the crew arrives. It's always better for makeup artists to get to the location ahead of the call time so that you can be set up and ready to go for when the model arrives. For me, being exactly 'on time' is the same as being late.

Plan for the unexpected

You never know what you might need, who you might be working with or what might happen on set, so always be ready for anything. When it comes to both models and makeup briefs, there can be changes at the last minute, so bring enough kit to be prepared, regardless of what you're asked to do.

Be organised, no exceptions

Whether you're working with Madonna or your neighbour, Mary, you should treat them the same way. Always get your kit ready the day beforehand, bring a selection of products in case your client is allergic to any particular brands, have your brushes ready and know exactly where you're heading to before you leave the house. I use a diary to stay organised – I always write down the location details, contact numbers and any other information I need to know.

Don't take it personally

Things happen. Mistakes get made. It was most likely not your fault and even if it was, you already know never to do it again so just move on. Learn from your mistakes and don't keep making the same ones.

If it doesn't directly affect you, don't get involved

Say the photographer and the stylist are having a shouting match on set: it's none of your business and I'd strongly recommend staying out of it. It's not your battle. This happened on a shoot I was working on a few years ago – I just kept the model distracted by telling her awful knock-knock jokes that I'd forgotten the punch lines to.

Be careful

Don't be too trusting of the people you're working with if you don't know them. Even though we all work in the same industry, you will still come across opportunists, so be aware. This particularly applies if you're offered a lift home at night from a crew member that you just met. It will probably be fine – but what if it isn't?

Look professional, but don't focus on your appearance alone

Making an effort in your appearance is important but, ultimately, the work you do is what really counts. Let me tell you a little story. When I was starting out, it was always emphasised to me how important appearance was. To be honest, I was taught that 'once you look great, even if you do a horrible job, you'll still get away with it'. Also, that 'you can flirt your way out of anything'. What a mentor, right?

On the first fashion shoot I ever assisted on, I was advised to wear high heels on set. I was told that flats are unsightly and that, without heels, you look like you aren't making any effort. As I was eager to impress, I wore a pair of four-inch heels. The only problem was that the shoot wasn't taking place in a studio: it was in about ten different locations all around Dublin city and the crew decided – because it was such a lovely day – that we should all walk to each set-up. See where I'm going with this? Don't forget that as well as those stupid shoes, I also had my entire kit to drag around behind me all day!

It was one of the worst decisions I've ever made. Because of the pain in my feet, I couldn't focus on what I was supposed to be doing. I was getting hot from the stress and annoyed at having to walk so far, and I genuinely lost all interest in the shoot by the end of the day. There are two things to take from this story:

- High heels are jerks and don't belong on set, unless they're on the feet of the model who's being photographed.
- When working on set, you need to wear something that is comfortable and allows you to jump over a wall if you need to.

Take all advice with a grain of salt

The story above makes it clear; not all the guidance you receive will be worth taking. In my career as a makeup artist I've experienced so much – both good and bad – but some of the biggest mistakes I've ever made were decisions taken on the advice of others. Remember that, sometimes, the people who talk the most know the least.

2.2 IDENTIFYING WHERE YOU'D LIKE TO WORK

When people think of makeup artists, the most common area of employment that springs to mind is a makeup counter. While, yes, this is one area we can work in, it's easy to miss all of the others. Know that for every ad you see in a magazine, every news reporter on the TV and (surprisingly) even almost every politician who appears at an event or interview, a makeup artist has been involved.

Some of the key fields that makeup artists work in are:

- **Fashion and beauty:** working with magazines, clothing brands and cosmetic companies.
- **Film and TV:** working in TV studios and on location for film.
- **Commercial:** working with large companies on advertising campaigns.
- **Client/bridal:** doing makeup for bridal parties, as well as occasion makeup. Usually based from a house or a studio.
- **Makeup counters:** working in a shop representing and selling a specific brand.

Some artists will only work in certain areas, while others work between all five. The work I do is a combination of all of them, except I don't work on a makeup counter. As I worked in retail before I got into makeup, I felt that I'd already done my time in the world of uncomfortable uniforms, ridiculous sales targets and grumpy managers. That's not to say that there's anything wrong with working on a counter, because there are a lot of amazing opportunities that only come from working for a brand. It's a great way to start off, as you gain experience working with clients, learn about products and build your confidence as an artist.

2.3 NETWORKING & MAKING THE RIGHT CONTACTS

It's vital that you get to know the industry you'd like to work in. Find out who the key players are and send each of them a well-phrased and spell-checked email. This is an area that will take some time to build confidence in but, I promise you, it does get easier. I still remember when I started out, making lists of every photographer, stylist, agency and designer in Dublin. Over a few weeks, I filled an entire A4 pad with names and contact details. As I sat down and attempted to compose legible emails, I tried hard to disguise my complete and utter terror and ultimately, my fear of rejection. It's scary, but it has to be done: you have to put yourself out there. Even if you don't feel confident, keep that as your own little secret.

So, you want to work in the fashion industry?

Getting familiar with this industry is as easy as looking through fashion magazines. I used to religiously scan through every Irish magazine each month, taking down the names of the team that worked on their photoshoots. I would then go home, look them up online and get in touch.

Your main focus should be on the photographers and stylists as they're usually the ones that will decide which makeup artist gets booked. So, get a notepad and pen, make a good cup of coffee, get comfy and start googling. On page one, list off all of the photographers who are working in the country at the moment, write down their names, email addresses and put them in order of who you would like to work with most at the top. Then move on to page two, doing the same for stylists. Another great resource is to look up agencies and see who they're representing, as those with representation will usually be the most highly regarded in the industry.

Now your contact lists are all made up – what happens now? Your shameless pretending-you're-not-terrified-of-rejection self-marketing needs to be dialled up to eleven. How about phrasing your email something a bit like this:

Hi [name],

I hope you're keeping well.

My name is [your name] and I'm a freelance makeup artist based in [location]. I've been following your work for some time and would love to collaborate, should you ever need a makeup artist.

You can view my portfolio on www.[yournamehere].com. I have also attached some of my most recent work to this email.

Looking forward to hearing from you soon,

Kindest Regards,
[Your name]
[Your phone number]

Keep it short and sweet, to the point and always include samples of your work as well as your contact details. I know what you're thinking: what happens if they don't reply? No big deal, just email them again. If you have a physical portfolio book I would also add that you would love to meet them for a coffee so they could have a look through your book. If they don't respond within two weeks, I would politely send them a follow-up email saying something like:

> Hi [name],
>
> *I hope you're having a great week so far. I just wanted to follow up on whether you got my email, below?*
>
> *Looking forward to hearing from you soon.*
>
> *Kindest Regards,*
> *[Your name]*
> *[Your phone number]*

I would genuinely keep emailing them on a fortnightly basis, until they respond. It sounds desperate, but you need to stand out and not give up. They could be receiving lots of emails from people just like you so you need to be the one that perseveres. When you're following up, always be nice and polite as you don't know what their circumstances are. They might be so busy that they haven't had the chance to reply yet. Always remember not to take things personally – it's just business, babe! In a similar sense, if you would like to work in the film industry, research who is heading up the makeup teams and get in touch with them.

A good tip, and something I always do, is to email the photographer and stylist the day after working with them, simply saying that it was lovely meeting them and you're looking forward to working with them again soon. It's good manners, it ensures that they have your contact details to hand and, should they want to work with you again, it leaves them with an extra-positive impression of you.

On one final note, I would add this: don't burn any bridges. The industry is small, everyone knows everyone and word gets around quickly. There is a limited number of magazines, so you can't risk getting onto the wrong side of any of the editors. So, mind your manners, watch what you say and always be professional, even when others aren't. How others behave is none of your business, but how you behave is.

2.4 BUILDING YOUR PORTFOLIO

A portfolio is a collection of images that represent your best work. Displayed on a website, in a book or preferably both, your work will 'sell' your skills more than any qualification or certificate ever will. That's why it's essential that you can demonstrate and showcase your best work by developing an accurate, up-to-date portfolio. You want your book to reflect your current skill level, your style and the quality of the service that you provide. It should show a diverse selection of makeup looks and only include the very best of your work. If you decide to go for a book, they should usually contain about 30 inserts with a hard cover, be A4 sized or larger and contain only images as no text is necessary. These books can be bought in most stationery shops as well as being available from specialist stores that can be found online. Whatever option you decide to go for make sure your images are easily removable should you want to update your work. I bought my portfolio book from a shop in London that produced handmade books. There are lots of different options to suit all budgets, so only spend what you can afford. When you're budgeting for it, remember that photo prints cost money, too: depending on your portfolio size, images can cost you anywhere from €5 to €15 each, depending on where you get them printed. If you're investing in an expensive book, make sure you get a case to protect it and prevent it from getting scratched.

I noticed that by having a portfolio book, it helped me to setup meetings with potential clients. I would mention in my email that some of my work is displayed on my website but my full portfolio of work is contained in my book should they like to meet me and look through it. Then once I meet with them, we can get to know each other and they can fall for my Irish charm.

To help keep the process simple, here's my main advice on building a makeup portfolio:

Test shoots

As I mentioned in an earlier section *(2.1: Industry Terms & Advice)*, test shoots are when a group of creatives come together to do a photoshoot. If you have a concept of something specific that you would like to create, get in touch with a team and see if they would be interested in collaborating with you. By working with different people, you will be able to create a diverse range of images for your portfolio that will ultimately lead to paid work down the line.

Only show your very best

Don't include any work that you're not 100 percent proud of. This goes beyond just the makeup – I've done many shoots where I loved what I did, but the styling or something about the model was just a bit 'off' that day, so I won't use that image. You have to have total confidence in your portfolio: if you don't, it will show. Remember, it's better to show one amazing image than ten not-so-great ones.

Avoid using multiple images from the same shoot

Only use the very best - it always looks stronger. If you include more than one image from the same look, make sure it's from a very different angle and helps to sell the overall look you created.

High-resolution images

When you're having images printed for your portfolio, only ever use high-resolution files (known as 'hi-res') as they will be crystal clear when printed. They are large, high-quality image files. The easiest way to tell if an image is hi-res is to open it on your computer and zoom right in. If the picture gets blurred or is hard to make out, it's a low-res file, but if the picture stays clear and you can make out every pore on the model's face, it's hi-res. You can also tell by opening the file information (or details) and checking the size of the file.

Think of your portfolio as a story

You'll hear people talk a lot about 'stories' in the fashion industry. For a fashion editorial, it's important that the themes are cohesive and you need to think the same way about your portfolio. Keep all similar looks together, start your book with natural makeup looks and build up to the most dramatic ones at the end.

Have a strong start and finish

It's very important that the first and last images of your book are really strong. If you're having a meeting and are showing your portfolio, chances are that they will stop on either of these pages to chat so make sure that they are both really strong and sell your skills.

A good model is key

Makeup artists usually don't have any say in which models are booked for jobs, but if you are putting together a test shoot for your portfolio, you will help to make the choice. You can apply the best makeup you've ever done and work with an amazing photographer, but if the model can't do her part, the whole shoot will be a waste of time. At the beginning of your career you will just need to gain experience, so the quality of the model doesn't matter quite as much, but as time goes on, you'll need to be more picky.

Know when to get rid of an image

If a look doesn't represent the quality of your work anymore, get rid of it. This can be hard – we all get emotionally attached to our work – but as time goes on and your skill level improves,you need that to be reflected in your portfolio, so always know if it's gotta go!

Never stop updating your work

You should never get to the point where you feel that your portfolio is 'finished'. As an artist, you should constantly be striving to improve your skills so never stop thinking up new ideas.

Back up everything

It's crucial that you backup your work in a few places. If you're solely reliant on your laptop and said laptop dies, so will you! Save all your portfolio files on your computer as well as on a separate hard drive. Hard drives are relatively cheap to buy and are available in a range of different memory sizes; getting two is also a good idea. After a photographer sends you the files from a photoshoot, save them directly onto your laptop, on to your hard drive and also online on the likes of Google Drive or Dropbox so the files are easily accessible at all times. Remember, as I always say, 'expect the worst, hope for the best'!

CV

Having an up-to-date CV is a good idea but it isn't as important as your portfolio. I have never once been asked for a CV, instead I have a biography on my website alongside my portfolio. That's usually all potential clients will want to see. If you are applying for a job on a makeup counter, a strong CV is vital. Depending on what the type of job is, you'll need to tailor your CV to that position so if it's a sales job, focus on your sales experience as that is what your potential employer will want to see. Make sure your CV is short, to the point and up-to-date. Also, always include a cover letter to show that you have made an extra effort and in it you can include an introduction, the job you are applying for and why your experience and skills match this role.

Tear sheets and PDFs

When things go to plan for you in your new career as a makeup artist, you'll hopefully have some of your work published in a magazine. Alongside your normal portfolio, it's important to keep a copy of all your published work: your 'tear sheets', as they're known in the industry. Keep a separate portfolio folder for these and, anytime you have some work published, buy two copies of the magazine, putting one copy of the images in your folder whilst keeping the other for safekeeping, should you ever lose this folder. Carefully cut out each page and insert them into the folder, keeping your very best work, such as magazine covers, to the front. My tear sheet portfolio is A4, which is the same size as most conventional magazines and has a hard, black cover with clear inserts. Books like these can be found in any good stationery shop and are available in a range of prices.

This might seem like a dream at this stage of your career, but dream big – if people have done it before, why can't you? I've always said that I'll get myself on a shoot for Italian Vogue one day, and I know it's achievable: other makeup artists work with that magazine all the time; I just need to find out how they got there.

Photographers and copyright

It's important to be respectful of photographers' work and to not edit or distribute their images without permission. For example, I hear from a lot of photographers that it's upsetting for them when someone posts one of their images on social media and adds a filter that completely changes the shot. Also if an image is posted online but the creative team who were responsible for making it aren't credited or tagged. Little things like this mightn't seem like a big deal at the time but, in a small industry, you need to be aware of what might cause friction with colleagues.

After a shoot, whether paid or unpaid, it can take a few weeks for the photographer to send out the images to the team. This could be because they're busy with work and haven't had time to edit the images just yet. Before shots are edited they're called 'raw' images – in general, these are of low quality and need to be worked on using editing software before they're released.

Hi-res images are very large files – too large to attach to an email. Instead, photographers will usually send you the files via Dropbox or WeTransfer. These are a fast and easy way to transfer large files and are both free to use. Once you get the images, remember to store them on a hard drive as well as on Google Drive, in case anything should happen to your computer.

If the photographer doesn't send you the images after a shoot, politely ask them if they could send them to you via email whenever they get a chance. Sometimes you may have to email a few times before you get a response, but regardless of how long it takes, always phrase your follow-up emails in a polite and friendly manner. Again, don't burn bridges – you could miss out on potential work in the future.

Published work and copyright

It's important to note that if you have worked on a photoshoot that is going to be published in a magazine, you cannot upload any pictures online until it's released. You may need to wait a few months in some circumstances and, to prevent any confusion on this matter, sometimes the photographer will wait until the publication's release before they send any images out to the team. As well as having the hi-res files sent to you, ask the magazine for page PDFs, as this file will display the shoot exactly as it appears in the magazine, including credits and captions.

2.5 GETTING YOUR NAME OUT THERE

Websites

A strong website that displays your work is an integral part of promoting yourself online. A few years ago, hiring someone to build you a website was a tedious, time-consuming and expensive task, but now it's easier than ever to make one yourself. First of all, you'll need to buy a domain name for your new website. This will be your website's address (or URL); for example, www.yournamehere.com. Keep your domain name simple and to the point – nothing too crazy or unidentifiable. Personally, I think just using your name is the strongest option and it will make it easier for potential clients to find you online. Some makeup artists will give themselves a different name but unless it's under a salon or brand name, I personally wouldn't recommend it. It can be quite tacky and cheapen the service you offer.

Domain names can be purchased through a wide variety of websites. Before you buy your new domain name, you'll need to double check that it is currently available. If the exact address you want to use isn't available, instead of '.com', why not go for '.net'? Domains are inexpensive and you can usually choose to pay monthly or annually. When purchasing your new domain, you will be given the option to add a corresponding email address: choose something simple, professional and short. For example, my domain is www.ciaraallen.net and my email address is info@ciaraallen.net.

Now you have your domain and professional email address setup, instead of getting someone to build you an expensive website from scratch, you can buy a template online. There are a number of websites that sell templates like Squarespace, Wordpress and Wix, and the good thing is that they can be changed at any time if you want something new.

Upload your work to the template site, link it to your new domain name and then you're ready to start building your empire.

Business cards

I would recommend keeping your business cards simple, timeless and minimal in terms of how much information you put on them. The ones I use now are plain, thick, white card with my name, phone number, email address and website in a simple black font – but I'll let you in on a funny story. When I was starting out all of those years ago, I got a little overly enthusiastic at the thought of having my own business cards. In a flurry of excitement that whirled me around like a banana in a blender, I hastily ordered a batch online; so hastily that, I forgot to put my phone number on them. Unfortunately, that wasn't even the worst of it. As I've already said, the most important thing about your business cards are that they are simple, timeless and minimal – but no one told me that.

So, what were my first ones like, you ask? Well they had a big skull on the front – and, on the back, said 'Ciara Allen, makeup artist: Not for the faint-hearted'. Hardly going to book bridal jobs with a motto like that, now was I! Learn from my mistakes and stick to the elegant basics.

Choosing a name and logo

When it comes to logos and business names, your decision will come down to personal preference, but I'm not a big fan of either. A lot of the time, artists will just generate a basic logo online (that often has lipstick spelling out their name) and it can look quite cheap. If you can afford it and really want a logo, contact a graphic designer and get one that represents your business in a professional way. But this is really an unnecessary bonus: just having your name in a clear and simple font makes a great impression and will cost you nothing.

2.6 SOCIAL MEDIA, BLOGGING AND DEALING WITH ONLINE TROLLS

It may sound ridiculous, but if your business isn't on social media it might as well not exist. Some people feel that they're making a point by not advertising online but, really, they're the only ones who are going to suffer when the work dries up. Businesses need to stay up-to-date with technology and customers love nothing more than being able to follow their favourite celebrities and brands online. People love to know what your favourite products are and see what goes on behind the scenes on photoshoots and TV shows: social media is a great way to build relationships with your followers.

While these online tools have given us a great opportunity to market ourselves to a wider audience, it's also an area you need to be careful in. It's important to understand that your personal and business social media accounts need to be separate. All that should be posted on your business accounts are things related to the work you're doing, the products you're loving, etc. Your potential clients don't need to see a drunken selfie taken at 2am outside a Burger King, with the hashtag #drunkanddontgiveadamn. Also, think twice before posting anything promoting a strong view on politics, religion, or other issues that could be seen as controversial and might potentially put clients off. The golden rule is 'always think before you post': ask, 'Is it relevant to my business?' or 'Could it potentially harm my business?' , and, if in doubt, leave it out. With technology advancing so rapidly each year, it's hard to imagine at what level social media will be in ten years' time.

At the moment, the key social media sites are Instagram, Facebook and Twitter. It's important to post every day and to interact with your followers as much as possible. Make sure your social media handles (AKA your usernames) relate clearly to you and are professional. For example, my Instagram handle is @ciaraallenmakeupartist. Pretty self-explanatory, right? Keep your username simple, professional and to the point.

You can also use social media to build relationships within the industry. For a start, it's good to follow other makeup artists in your area. It's very easy for people to feel competitive with each other, but I just think there's no need. We're all trying to follow a similar path, but we each have a unique style and personality. Reaching out and supporting other artists will only benefit you in the long run **and by opening up a dialogue and complimenting others on their work, you might just get the same back in return.** They may also pass on any work that they're unable to take on, so I'd strongly recommend making friends in the industry – not enemies. Also, you never know who you might meet on social media and you may even make a few friends along the way.

Use your pages to let everyone know what you're up to. If you or your work has been featured in a magazine or you appeared on a TV show, make sure all of your followers know about it. As you most likely can't afford to pay someone to do your marketing for you, you need to take it on yourself and get good at it, fast. You need to be proud of what you've achieved in your career to date, to show that you're involved in the industry and that you're on a mission to be one of the best artists in the country (dare I say, the world?)! Be professional but friendly when you interact with your followers – you'll never really know who is checking out your work but isn't necessarily following your account. I've seen some huge makeup brands following my videos on Instagram, so always be aware that people who could help further your career might be watching so keep your posts related to your business.

Tag makeup brands and companies that you like in pictures that you post to help get your work out there. For example, if you did a beauty shoot and you mainly used MAC Cosmetics products, tag them in your picture and include a #MACCosmetics hashtag in your post in the hope that someone from the brand will see it. Hashtags are great to get your work seen by other makeup lovers, so always include some relevant ones.

On a final note, don't get involved in any internet drama that could potentially harm your business. If it doesn't concern you, then it doesn't concern you. Repeat this mantra: if it doesn't concern you, then it doesn't concern you.

Blogging

If you're thinking of starting a blog, I would consider asking yourself why you want to. Is it because you love writing, reviewing products and sharing your opinions? If you answered 'yes' to all three of these then I would recommend you go for it. If you only want to blog to get free products, I think you could be doing something more productive with your time instead: blogging takes up quite a lot of time and it's a big commitment.

I always say to people that if you don't want to blog, don't blog. If you don't feel like posting, don't post. Unless it's your job and you have a contractual agreement with a person or a company to post about specific things at agreed times, you have no one to answer to except yourself. It's all on your terms – never forget it.

Internet trolls

A troll is a very unhappy person who scours the internet waiting for an opportunity to strike. The more they bring others down, the better they feel about their own lives. My other half always says, 'don't feed the trolls' – and it's so important to always remember that. The more attention you give them, the bigger they get and the worse they become. Instead, just ignore them; they don't deserve a moment of your time.

I once had a woman troll my business Facebook page. She left me a horrible comment saying that I made my business feeding on other people's insecurities and that what I did was disgusting. I was devastated: all that I ever try to do is empower women. How could she possibly think I was trying to do the opposite? I made a silly mistake: I replied. I wasn't rude – I just tried to set her straight and prove that what she was saying wasn't true – but I forgot the cardinal rule, 'don't feed the trolls'. A troll will never admit that they are wrong or stand down. A very unpleasant back-and-fourth ensued and last for about 30 minutes, and that night she won: she sucked me in, she hurt my feelings and I paid her all of the attention that she wanted. Every comment she wrote kept getting worse and I just didn't know what to do. I stepped away from my phone, realised that this woman obviously had huge issues in her own life and took a deep breath. I commented one last time: 'Thanks ___, take care'. I deleted all of her horrible comments, blocked her and vowed never to make the same mistake again.

Don't even try to convert the trolls: it isn't worth the effort and they're too full of hate to ever see the world in a positive light.

2.7 ADVERTISING

The days of advertising in newspapers and magazines are not quite over, but it's certainly not as relevant as it used to be. While they can still definitely help your business, they can be quite expensive and mightn't necessarily reach your target market. For a more direct and cost-effective approach, why not target the people near your location who are looking for a makeup artist online? This can be done through Google AdWords or social media advertising. If you place an ad through Google AdWords, when a potential client searches for something relevant to your ad, it will come up on the first page of the search engine. You can select a 'Pay per Click' option, which means that you will only be charged every time someone clicks on your ad. If no one clicks, you won't be charged. The more you pay, the higher your ad will come up in searches, so plan a daily budget that you can afford, decide what you want your ad to say and the geographical location you want to target. If you want to try this route, simply sign up for a Google AdWords account, fill in the details and you're ready to go.

With social media use thriving across all age groups, it's a great way to advertise directly to your target market. You can do this through a number of platforms, the biggest currently being Instagram and Facebook. Through both sites, you can choose the parameters of your target market, down to their gender, age and location. Simply decide on how much you want to spend, how long you want your ads to run for and what you want them to say.

2.8 EMAIL & PHONE ETIQUETTE

How you conduct yourself via email is very important. When dealing with unpleasant people, I would always recommend going for the 'kill them with kindness' approach: you have to approach situations, both good and bad, with professionalism and patience. I always say, 'Never write anything that you wouldn't want someone to publicly quote you on', and it's good to keep that in mind. Where something is said verbally, it can be easily forgotten, but once it's in writing, it's a very different story. Everything can be saved as a screenshot, and your reputation can be destroyed in a matter of seconds if you say the wrong thing. Sometimes what you really want to say and what you should say are two very different things.

I always try to respond to all emails I get within 24 hours. I get really annoyed when people take a long time to respond to my emails so, to combat that, I always respond as quickly as I can. I suggest starting all your emails on a friendly and positive note, along the lines of what I've included below:

Hi [name],
I hope you're keeping well.
Thanks so much for your email – it's so lovely to hear from you.

Congratulations on your big day. When did you get engaged?
What's your Fiancée's name?
I've just checked my diary and at the moment I am available on [date of wedding] so I've provisionally booked you in.
I've included a quote below:

- €XX per person on the day.
- €XX per person for a trial.
- €XX travel expenses.

*In total it would be €XX and I require a 50 percent booking deposit
to secure the date.
Any questions, please don't hesitate to get in touch.*

*Kindest regards,
[Your name]*

Voicemail

It's pretty self-explanatory, but make sure your business line has an appropriate voicemail: one that's short and professional. All you have to say is, 'Hi there, sorry I missed your call. Please leave your name, number and a quick message and I'll get back to you as soon as I possibly can'.

STAGE 3:

KIT ESSENTIALS & SETTING UP A STATION

Mark all of the products in your kit, as well as your makeup brushes, with a dot of brightly coloured nail varnish. Should you be working alongside other artists on a shoot, you will be able to tell which products belong to you.

3.1 MAKEUP STATION SETUP & LIGHTING

How you setup your station will vary according to your own personal preference and the kind of job you're working on that day. My station is functional for the way I work, as well as hygienic and practical. Only take out what you actually plan on using, as this will save time setting up and packing up afterwards.

You should always be looking for some natural light, so setting up beside a window is preferable, as is having a medium-to-large table for you to put your products on. If you're working in a studio, they will usually have a makeup area, but the quality of this area can vary widely. If you setup in an area that is starved of natural light, you always run the risk of using a shade of foundation that isn't quite right. The more you get to know skin-tones the less this will happen, but if you're unsure, I'd always bring the client or model out into brighter light, just to double check that everything is perfect. Also observe and note the way that different skin tones look under artificial light and how it can change the way the makeup looks – usually for the worse. If you're doing a client's makeup in their house, you'll need to alter your setup to suit the furniture they have available (and please don't make demands for furniture they don't have). Just keep it in mind that you always need to be as close to a window with as much natural light as possible with a table to put your kit on.

If you drive, I strongly recommend getting a fold-up high chair to keep in the back of your car, which you can use for makeup appointments that take place outside a studio. These chairs are inexpensive and will generally last – depending, of course, on how well you treat them. Doing makeup on a client while they sit on a small chair is very unpleasant: you won't be able to see what you're doing, they'll need to arch their neck up to help your visibility, your back will get sore and you'll be counting down the minutes until your appointment is over so you can finally stand up straight. An investment of around €25 will save you having to deal with all of this. Don't feel that you have to get a fancy director's chair with your logo on the back, as that will cost you more money. Keep that cash for that new highlighter you've wanted for ages instead.

Skincare *Skin* *Eyes*

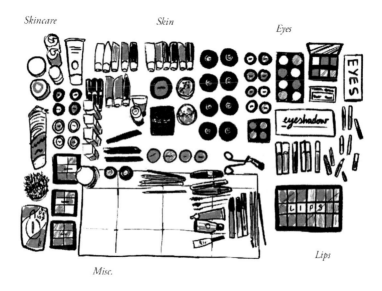

Lips

Misc.

When setting up my station, I want to line up the products in the order that I'll need them. This helps to keep things organised and tidy before the chaos begins. Firstly, I'll clean the table with a wipe and put down two tissues. Someone once told me that makeup artists need to use couch roll (the paper that a doctor or beautician puts over a bed before you lie down on it), but this is completely unnecessary, not to mention impractical: Couch roll is quite bulky, expensive and would take up a lot of room in your kit. I use small travel packs of tissues, like the ones you can throw in your handbag.

Here are the steps I follow to setup my station:

1. I start by laying down two clean tissues. This is where I will put down my brushes once I've used them.

2. I get two nappy bags out: one for rubbish, like used cotton buds and pads, and one for my used brushes to go into when I'm finished with them. On the tissue, I lay out clean cotton buds, pads and unused disposable mascara wands. I put a pack of baby wipes on the table as I'll use them the wipe down my hands when needed and to clean the products before I pack them up at the end.

3. The first products I place on the table are skincare. Before I start the makeup, I do a quick cleanse so these products include cleanser, toner, eye-makeup remover (should they have any old makeup still on their skin or sleep around their eyes that needs removing), liquid exfoliator, moisturiser and lip balm.

4. Next, I line up the foundation I plan to use and arrange them with lightest colour at the front leading to the darkest at the back This makes it quick and easy for me to find the shade I need.

5. Then I line up my concealers and under-eye illuminators in order of lightest to darkest.

6. I keep my blushers, highlighters and bronzers together because I apply them all around the same time.

7. Next, I lay out a selection of powders – loose, as well as pressed – in colour order.

8. I keep all of the eye products together so everything from brow pencils, mascaras, eye primers and eyeshadows are all in the same area. I only display the eyeshadow palettes I actually plan to use, and open the ones I use the most.

9.   Last are the lips, so I set out my lipstick palettes, lip liners and
     liquid lipsticks together at the end of the table.

Working this way means that I always know generally where each
product is. If you're working in a confined space, I recommend keeping
your products in their clear plastic bags and laying them out in the order
you'll use them. This will save both time and space.

On a final note, make sure you put the used brushes away from your
last client before you start with the next one, change the tissue and empty
the rubbish bag. You don't want your next client to feel that they're
getting a different experience to your first client, so keep your standards
high at all times. Think of what you would expect if you were the client
and always stay in that frame of mind, regardless of how long you've
been in the industry.

3.2 BRUSH BELT

The ways that artists like to store their brushes can vary but I like to keep mine in a brush belt. Where most people wear these belts around their hips, I wear mine across my body, like a soldier wearing a bandolier, and this helps me to see all of my brushes clearly.

Here's what I have in my brush belt:

Makeup brushes

Ground-breaking stuff, isn't it? I bet you needed a book to tell you that! Just like my station, I keep my brushes in order of how I use them. I also keep similar brushes together, e.g. foundation and concealer brushes together. I couldn't even tell you how many brushes I stuff into my poor belt but I always want to be sure, regardless of what happens, that I'll have clean ones ready to go.

Hand sanitiser and breath spray

In the front pouch of my brush belt, I keep a small bottle of both so I always have them close by. If I've had a quick coffee just before my client arrives, I'll always use a mint breath spray so as not to pass the whiff of caffeine on.

Powder puff

While I don't use these all of the time, I find that they're so handy to have in a makeup emergency – perfect for when you need to apply a lot of powder quickly or to do a touch-up before a bride walks down the aisle.

Spatula

While you can take a cream product out of it's packaging for use with the end of your brush handle, a spatula is handy to keep everything hygienic and is also great for mixing colours.

Nail scissors

It might surprise you but one of the things I get asked for most on shoots, or even when I'm with clients, is scissors. They're great for trimming lashes and cutting the tags off clothes.

Pencil sharpener

It's always important to have one on hand so you can keep your lip and eye pencils sharp and clean.

3.3 SKIN

Putting together a makeup kit is possibly one of the most stressful things to consider (as well as to pay for) when you decide to become a makeup artist. Makeup is expensive. Good quality makeup can be even more expensive. You'll need to have a kit that will cater to a range of different clients, as well as to a variety of different types of work.

This isn't a quick process. When I first started out, I wasted about €2,000 (that I put on a credit card) buying products that I thought were 'cool', like glitters, bright pigments and paints. Nothing practical. What I didn't know was that I would literally never use any of it and instead ended up giving a lot of it away so it was money (that I didn't even have yet) down the drain. Over time I learned what I actually need, what I'll actually use and what is really worth paying that bit extra for.

Below I've compiled a simple list of skincare products that I couldn't do my job without. Good quality skincare is beyond important and is worth investing in because if you don't have a well-prepped base to work with, whatever makeup you apply onto the skin won't sit right. You never know – they might help you save the day on a shoot if the model shows up in dire need of a face mask.

Below is what I carry in my core skincare kit. I specifically haven't mentioned any particular brands because products get discontinued far too often and I don't want to break your heart.

Cream cleanser for all skin types
I start off each makeup with a full cleanse, so this is the first step.

Toner for sensitive skin
I use this to remove the cleanser or to do a quick refresher on the skin.

If you have a bit extra to spend, I would also get a toner specifically designed for oily skin.

Pore refiner

If someone has problematic pores, unless you treat them, they will be a complete nightmare and even the most expensive foundation on the market won't sit right. A pore refiner should be applied to the troublesome area before foundation to help improve the skin's texture.

Face masks

This sounds excessive, but I use them on photoshoots all the time. I like to apply them to the model, then let her have her hair done so the mask can sit on the skin for a while and do what it needs to do. This can also be a nice touch for brides on the morning of their wedding if they want some extra attention and you have some time to spare.

Exfoliator

I recommend having two different types: a rough scrub as well as a liquid lotion. An exfoliator helps to get rid of any dry skin and helps to smooth out uneven texture. A quick exfoliate before you start the makeup will save you a whole lot of heartbreak later on. If your client has flaky, dry skin, makeup will sit unevenly and get stuck in the cracks, so treat it beforehand instead of trying to fix it afterwards.

An under-eye primer

This is mainly for use on mature skin and works well to temporarily smooth out any fine lines and wrinkles before applying any makeup. Make sure your clients understand that its effect is, unfortunately, only temporary!

Lip balm

Now, not just any lip balm: you need a really good one that actually works. I like using a balm that is quite thick so you can apply heavily to the lips when you're doing your skincare prep, before applying any makeup. This gives it some time to sit on the lips while you do the rest of the makeup; you can then remove it with a cotton bud just before you apply lipstick at the very end.

Lip scrub

If someone has really dry lips, whatever lipstick you put on top of them will just highlight the dry skin, but by giving them a quick scrub, it will get rid of any flaky skin and get them ready for lipstick.

Moisturiser

A good moisturiser is so vital: for that reason I carry a few different ones in my kit. If you can only afford to get one, get a cream that will cater for all skin types. I like to apply moisturiser with my hands so you can warm up the cream before application and then massage it into the skin.

Serum

Think of this as a moisturiser on steroids. While a moisturiser will just tackle the top layer of skin, a serum penetrates a few layers down so it will make sure the skin is thoroughly hydrated. They tend to be a bit more expensive, so start off with a good moisturiser and then you can save up for a serum over time.

3.4 FOUNDATIONS & CONCEALERS

Foundation

Possibly one of the most daunting areas for makeup artists is building up a selection of foundations that will cater for all types of jobs, as well as for all skin tones and types. I still get the fear that I don't have enough, even though I carry around fifteen different types of foundations. In my opinion, this is an area where the concept of 'you get what you pay for' heavily applies, but in theory, three types of foundation will get you through almost any situation:

Liquid foundation for all skin types

Now this is totally down to personal preference, but I prefer a liquid foundation with a natural dewy finish. You can keep the coverage light or build it up for a heavier look if need be, as well as being able to mix it with a moisturiser for a really light coverage that can be used for male makeup. If you can only afford a few shades, get the lightest, a medium and a dark tone so you can mix them to cater for all skin tones. In general, I usually go for yellow-toned products.

Long-lasting foundation

These types of foundations tend to have a high powder content, which is why they last longer on the skin. They're great for weddings, on clients with oily skin and to help makeup last a long time in a hot climate. Again, go for two to three shades and then mix them to suit your client.

A powder-compact foundation

Powder foundations are great if you have to do a makeup look in a very short amount of time, as well as being total lifesaver for touch-ups on photoshoots. Sometimes the model might accidentally rub her nose without thinking and, in doing so, wipe off some of the makeup you spent an hour expertly applying, just before the photographer starts shooting. Instead of having to mess around with a liquid foundation and then a separate powder, you can go straight in with powder foundation on a sponge or a fluffy brush and fix the area up in less than ten seconds.

Other options

As time goes on, it's a good idea to branch out into other types of foundation for your kit, but don't ever take a gamble on one without trying it on yourself first. Good foundations can be expensive but it's an investment, as some cheaper products can be a total nightmare to work with. With other makeup products, like mascara or lipstick, you can get away with cheaper options, but for foundation, I really feel that the better the quality, the easier your job will be.

Concealer

You can keep it pretty simple with concealers. I mainly use two different types:

For around the eye area

I like to use a liquid concealer, gently applied with a soft brush or my finger. As the skin around the eyes is very delicate, you want to use a lightweight product with good, long-lasting coverage. Anything too heavy will simply exacerbate any fine lines and wrinkles, which is the opposite of what your client wants.

For blemishes

This should be a heavier, cream concealer that has stronger coverage and good staying power. I would usually apply this type of product with my fingers or a tiny synthetic brush to get the product right on the blemish without covering the surrounding areas of 'good' skin.

3.5 POWDERS

Face powders are an important product to have in your kit as it's used to set the makeup in place and also to get rid of excessive shine. I carry about five different types of powders in my kit, which are all useful for different reasons. Here are my top picks:

Loose, invisible powder

Great for using around the eye area and to set face makeup. It usually comes in a wide range of shades and I would usually use translucent (which has no colour), light, medium and dark.

Blot powders

These are a heavier type of product that help to get rid of shine for long periods of time. They're great for photoshoots when the set is strongly lit; for theatre, because of the strong lighting; and also for TV, which can be shot in a harshly lit studio. I find blot powders are best applied with a sponge and would mainly use three shades: light, medium and dark.

High definition powder

These powders have a really fine texture and they're great for TV as they don't show up on the skin in HD. It's important to know that they don't work well for flash photography as they contain titanium dioxide, which causes flashback when applied in large amounts so just use them sparingly for a client who will be on TV.

Blusher

I could literally write a whole book just about blushers because I love them so damn much. They're one of those products that even if you carry 63 of them in your kit, you'll pretty much always use the same two or three. I'd say I carry around 30 different blushers but I have my favourites, which I use 99 percent of the time which are from Stila, Ben Nye and MAC Cosmetics.

I'd recommend making up a blusher palette with a few of your favourite colours in it so you don't end up searching through your entire kit looking for one individual shade on every job. Palettes will make your life so much easier and will keep everything as compact as possible. This also makes products easier to find in a hurry or on a stressful photoshoot. Cream blushers are a favourite of mine as they look really beautiful when softly applied to the cheeks. Again, just go for two or three shades, or, even better, opt for a cream blusher palette.

Bronzer

It's worth investing in a good bronzer as they're the type of product that you'll have for a long time unless you a) drop it, or b) it smashes in your kit (and you're left devastated and questioning everything you care about in this world). I use a cream bronzer as well as a powder one and mainly use a light as well as a dark shade. I'm not a big fan of shimmery bronzer as they can look grubby on camera, so instead I keep them matte.

Highlighter

Over the last few years, the beauty industry has gone completely crazy for highlighters. Available in liquids, creams and powders, the choice on every makeup counter is truly the stuff of dreams (or nightmares when you can't afford to buy them). Highlighters really boil down to your own personal preference but I would recommend having a liquid one that can be used on limbs for photoshoots or shows, a cream one in two or three different shades for the face and a powder one so you can amp the highlight up to a dangerously high 11*. My advice would be to go for a powder highlighter that is very finely milled so it doesn't look heavy on the skin, and also nothing too glittery. (*Spinal Tap reference).

3.6 EYES

Brows

There are so many different brow products on the market these days – pencils, gels, creams and brow mascaras – that it's totally overwhelming trying to choose which ones to go for. In general, I like to keep things simple and, even though I carry around 12 different brow products in my kit, I always use the same few without fail which are from Benefit, Smashbox and MAC Cosmetics. With brows, so much is just down to the type of brows you want to create, as well as what type of brows your client wants. Generally, using a gel product will give you a stronger effect, whereas a pencil, when applied carefully, will give you a lighter and more natural look. I mainly use a brow pencil in light and dark shades, as well as brow mascaras to fix the hair in place.

Mascara

People are always quite surprised that I use budget-friendly brands of mascara, but so many of them are better than the luxury-branded ones and don't come up with an obscene price tag. You'll also need to restock mascaras quite often, so if you can get a great one for half the price, why not! I always use black mascara on the upper lashes and sometimes opt for brown mascara on the lower ones, as this helps to give a softer look. The main types of mascaras I would recommend are a waterproof one for brides, a volumising one to give the illusion of thicker lashes, a brown mascara and a lengthening mascara. Also, an eyelash curler is a must-have.

Liner

I would recommend having a liquid liner, a gel liner in a few different shades and some pencil eyeliners in a few different colours. The ones you'll use the most often will be brown and black, so resist buying the lime green as it might lay in your kit untouched for about a decade until it comes back into style.

Eyeshadow

This is an area of complete torture because, as each brand releases a new palette, your head will know that you don't really need it but your heart will already be entering your card details online. I'll admit that I have so many palettes that I carry around with me but without fail I pretty much always go back to my favourite, which is a palette I put together myself. As a general rule, I'd recommend having a selection of nudes, medium-toned browns, greys, dark browns, black and a few shimmer shadows.

As time goes on you can build up your colour selection but when starting out I'd recommend keeping it really simple, neutral and, dare I say it, practical.

Cream eyeshadows are also great to have and, again, I would stick to a neutral, a brown and a dark shade for starting out and then expand when you can afford to. Also, an eyeshadow primer is great to have in your kit and one in a neutral or translucent shade will come in a very useful for a range of different makeup looks.

3.7 LIPS

Lipstick

The selection of lipsticks currently on the market are slightly intimidating when trying to decide which ones you should carry in your kit. With a mixture of different textures and finishes, you need to choose wisely if you're on a budget, so listen to your head not your heart on this one. I'd strongly recommend putting your most used lipsticks into a palette so they're easy to find when you need them (see my tips on making palettes and depotting in section 3.8). There's nothing worse than looking for a particular shade in a hurry in a kit stuffed with identical looking lipsticks. Over the years, I've made up four different lip palettes for my kit; each contains 25 lipsticks and are labelled so I know where each shade is. I have one palette dedicated to nude and natural shades, one for reds in a variety of different tones, one for burgundies and purples and then, finally, a wild-card palette that contains everything from green to black for those 'just in case' moments! (I've never used them just yet, but you never know, right?)

It's a good idea to have a handful of nude lipsticks that cover a pale pink, a pale peach, a brown pink and a neutral pink. For stronger colours, I'd recommend having a warm matte red, a blue-toned matte red and a deep burgundy. Of course, it's great to have a few options of each shade, but keep it simple in the beginning. I'm also currently a fan of liquid lipsticks as they're super long-lasting for weddings and for long photoshoots so I carry a few (25+) shades of those as well.

Gloss

I don't use gloss all that often but I do carry a few different ones just in case it's needed. A clear gloss is fantastic to have available, as you can put it on top of any shade and it will work beautifully. As you expand your kit you can add coloured glosses but at the beginning, there's not much need.

Lip liner

I have such a devotion to lip liners, as they're great for correcting an uneven lip shade and for cleaning up the lip line after applying lipstick. In general, you want to go for liners that are creamy in texture, as dry pencils will pull the skin, which can feel quite unpleasant for your client. In terms of colours, go for a light pink, a peach, a red and a dark burgundy and add more shades into the mix over time.

3.8 DEPOTTING, PALETTES, LABELLING & RESTOCKING

Recently I've finally realised that the size of my kit was getting out of control – to the point that I joke that I specifically took up weightlifting just so I could carry it around. There's definitely some truth in that, though: after a particularly long day shooting, lifting my kit into the car requires a great deal of effort and concentration. Sometimes I wish I had an army of assistants just like Pat McGrath – apparently, she carries around about 60 suitcases of makeup. Can you imagine trying to check those in at the airport? If you're hoping to travel with work, even shorter distances, you'll need to take a serious look at your makeup kit and figure out how to make it as compact as possible. Here are a few of my top tips:

Depotting

This has quickly become a kind of religion among makeup artists, maybe even a rite of passage. Depotting involves taking a product out of its original packaging and putting it into a smaller and more compact container. The heaviest products to carry in your kit are usually the ones in glass packaging, such as liquid foundations, so buy some small plastic bottles (which can be bought online from makeup supplies stores) and empty half the foundation into each bottle. Not only are you avoiding carrying the entire product around with you but you're leaving the heavy glass packaging behind as well. I know that doesn't sound like much, but when you're carrying 30–40 glass bottles in your kit, you'll feel the difference. The way I look at it is that I want to carry as many of my favourite products as possible but avoid having a kit that weighs more than my own bodyweight. This can also be done for your core skincare kit by buying some small pots and getting organised.

Palettes

As I mentioned in section 3.4, individual eyeshadows are a total nightmare to find in your makeup kit, so stick them into palettes wherever you can. Where possible, it's good to take the eyeshadow pan out of the packaging, put a magnet on the bottom of it and then put it into a large magnetic palette (these are available online). I'll confess, though – I don't actually use magnets; I just superglue them onto the palette. Yes, I know that I won't be able to take them out when they're empty, but to be honest, the effort of having to buy magnets seems like a total pain to me, so I just glue them down and hope for the best. Obviously you don't have to do this, but if you think like me, just go for it!

As well as foundations and eyeshadows, I also depot the majority of my cream blushers and lipsticks into palettes. This saves the effort of having to carry hundreds of lipstick tubes around with me and, as with the eyeshadows, it makes it easier to see what colour options you have without having to look very far.

To depot the lipstick, you'll need the following, as well as a grown-up to supervise if you're either clumsy or under the age of 18 (I didn't get a Blue Peter badge for nothing):

- A small metal spoon.
- A candle.
- An empty lipstick palette.
- Lipsticks.
- Baby wipes and a cup of water.
- A steady hand and a bit of patience.

In the palettes I use, you can fit about half a melted lipstick into each well. Lay down some newspaper in case you make a mess, get an old metal spoon, a cup and wear some old clothes in case there are any spills. Cut off half of the bullet, put it onto a metal spoon and hold it over the candle for about 10 seconds. The lipstick will melt very quickly, so keep a close eye on it. Do be careful that you don't leave the spoon over the flame for too long as you risk burning the lipstick.

From an artistic point of view, it's very satisfying watching all of the colours melt! Once the lipstick has melted into a liquid with no lumps, carefully pour it into the well. Put the spoon into a cup of cold water for a few seconds and then wipe it clean with a wipe. The lipstick will turn solid in a few minutes so leave it to set, try to resist sticking your fingers in it and move on to the next shade. An obvious tip, but something I actually forgot about the first time I did this, is to keep note of which shades you have put into which wells, so you can make labels for them afterwards. For the remainder of the lipsticks left in the tubes, keep them stored in a safe place so that when you need to refill your palette, you know exactly where to look.

I actually find making lipstick palettes quite therapeutic. I like to keep similar colours together and place them in order of lightest to darkest. For example, my nude lip palette is home to about 25 different lipsticks and I've laid them out so that the first shade is the lightest flesh tone, followed by a slightly darker one and so on. I like to take a bit of time planning which colours I'll put where, so it has a bit of a colour story. You'll want a palette that will inspire you when you're on a melter of a 14-hour shoot or you have a ridiculously hard-to-please client.

Labelling

I, like most human beings born in the 1980s have lusted after a label maker ever since I was a child. And dreams really can come true! When I started organising my makeup kit, I finally had a justification to buy one. I looked around online for the perfect machine – and by that, I mean the cheapest. I checked all the usual haunts – Amazon, eBay, etc. – but they were all super expensive. My hope started to fade. I was preparing for heartbreak and possibly a future hand-writing labels, when something amazing happened: I found one in a local electrical shop for only €20. I now use these labels for everything from my skincare products and foundation to lipstick and cream-blusher palettes and I recommend you do also.

Restocking

Keeping your makeup kit stocked can be both an act of pure love and complete torture. I've learned to always expect the unexpected, think ahead as much as you can (or as much as you can afford) and be aware of your key products and when they're nearly empty.

The main things you'll run out of are:

- Cotton pads.
- Cotton buds.
- Small packs of tissues.
- Baby wipes.
- Mascara wands.
- Makeup sponges.
- Baby shampoo (or whatever you use to wash your makeup brushes).

For cotton pads, cotton buds, tissues and baby wipes, I usually find the best deals are in large supermarkets. You want good quality, of course, but keeping costs down in a business is vital for its survival. Baby wipes are often on special offer so keep your eyes peeled for a good deal – I'll usually buy as many as I can carry. I also have a 'stock wardrobe' where I store things like this, which I draw on to restock my kit as needed.

Mascara wands are really expensive if you buy them in salon supply shops – the last time I checked they were €5 for 20 wands (making them 25c each), which is ridiculous. Instead, I buy mine online directly from China – I've done so for years. Have a good look around online for the cheapest ones. A lot of companies offer free shipping, which is great, but do take note that it can sometimes take one to two months for delivery and place your order well in advance. Makeup sponges can also be bought online, in advance for next to nothing, so do your research before you spend €30 on one sponge.

The products you carry in your kit are unique to you and what you like to use. I have my go-to products that I'd be really stuck without, and I always try and think ahead to make sure I'll never run out of them. If my favourite foundation is still half full (not half empty – I'm an eternal optimist), I'm already aware that I need to get another one as soon as I can. I mightn't need it for a few weeks, even months, but I feel better knowing that I have a spare one should I need it. If you leave it until the bottle is completely empty, you risk not having it when you really need it so save yourself the stress and plan ahead.

I go through a lot of mascara and always like to stock up on my favourites for when I'll need them. If you can get an offer when buying in bulk, even better. I don't use false lashes that much but I always have them, just in case. In general (depending on my mood), I tend to favour individual lashes over strips because you have a bit more control of the overall look that you're creating. They also tend to be a bit more on the subtle side.

Building up your kit is a long and extremely expensive process and even though I've been building mine for the last seven years, I still always want to add new things to it. It's like a painting that's never quite finished; you keep going back to add a little more to it. The best advice I could give you is to never leave anything to the last minute if you can avoid it and remember, you can never be too organised.

3.9 STORING YOUR KIT

Cases

How you decide to carry your makeup kit around with you is a personal choice but I'm here to spout some wisdom so do grab a seat, put your phone on silent and pay attention.

When I first started out, I was determined to own one of those beauty cases that are stackable and are on two wheels. I remember paying €150 for one (yes, that's for a case with nothing in it)! I bought it thinking that I was so damn divine and quickly found out that it was the most impractical purchase I'd ever made. Sure, the case might look nice from the outside, but in terms of lugging it around with you on photoshoots, it's a complete nightmare. Even though the cases look big, you'll be amazed at how little you can fit in them. After I brought it home, I brought it up to my room and introduced it to my makeup kit, carefully putting each product into its new home. But in the two years that I owned that case, it never left my house until I sold it to a beautician. It was difficult to wheel around, it was unfathomably heavy and was a total waste of money. If I just crushed your dreams I do apologise, but if I don't tell you the truth, who will?

The less glamorous – but more practical – approach is to store and transport your kit in a four-wheeled hard suitcase. The four wheels are vital so you can push the case along instead of pulling it, which will save your arms from getting tired. A hard case is important so your products won't get damaged if you're travelling on an airplane: you'll have to check in your makeup kit as it won't fit in the overhead. I'd recommend getting a case that isn't too 'jazzy'-looking: opt for a plain black one to keep things simple and avoid drawing attention to the contents. Before I drove, I used to wheel my cases everywhere on public transport; I would walk so far that the wheels would wear down every few months. Now that I drive, the cases last a lot longer but it's definitely worth spending a bit of money to make sure you get one that won't fall apart.

Inside your case

In my kit, I have all my products organised within an inch of their lives in clear, plastic cosmetics bags. These bags come in a range of sizes and styles and are usually very cheap to buy. My kit is organised as follows:

- Large skincare bag.
- Large hygiene bag, containing mascara wands, cotton buds, wipes, etc.
- Large foundation bag.
- Large eyeshadow bag with palettes as well as individual eye products, such as mascaras and gel liner.

- Medium-sized powder bag, containing face powders and bronzers.
- Medium-sized blusher bag.
- Medium-sized highlighter bag.
- Medium-sized lipstick bag for palettes and glosses.
- Small concealer bag.
- Small eyeliner bag.
- Small lip liner bag.
- Small nail polish bag.

I also have a few miscellaneous bags, but in general that's how I keep my kit organised. I want to know that regardless of which product I need, I know exactly where to find it. By starting off organised, not only will you look more professional on photoshoots but you'll also feel more put together and ready for anything.

3.10 RULES OF HYGIENE & DISPOSABLES

I believe that hygiene is of the utmost importance and as makeup artists we need to take it very seriously. If you're working in an unhygienic manner you are a risk to public health and your clients deserve much better. By working with dirty products and brushes, you can not only put at risk your clients' health, but also your reputation in the industry. Everything from cold sores to eye infections and skin irritations can be a direct result of bacteria-ridden tools and products that haven't been sanitised properly (if ever). So here's my guide to keeping clean:

Brushes

You should never use the same makeup brushes on multiple clients without washing them in between. You risk spreading everything from cold sores to conjunctivitis. If you're working with one set of brushes, get a good quality anti-bacterial brush cleaner and take a few minutes between each client to wash them properly before starting on the next face. Also, if you drop a brush on the floor, it's dirty, so don't put it back into your belt or, even worse, use it on your client.

Surgical spirit can be your saviour if you need a quick fix but, personally, I don't like using it in between clients. If you do use it to clean your brushes, be careful if it's undiluted, as it may kill all of the bacteria but will also leave your client with watery eyes and irritated skin. Some artists recommend mixing 50 percent distilled water with 50 percent surgical spirit to dilute it down and make it more usable. You can also put this mixture in a handy spray bottle to carry around with you in your kit. I wash my brushes with baby shampoo, baby oil and water. I will only use surgical spirits if I've worked on a client who has had a cold sore or some type of skin infection. I would also never actually put my brushes directly on to an area of infection, opting for a cotton bud instead. Even though my brushes never actually touch the affected area, I would never want to take the risk so I sterilise everything just in case. When I'm washing my brushes at home after that client, I'll put some surgical spirits on a tissue, rub each of my brushes thoroughly into the tissue, including the handles, and then wash with baby shampoo as normal. Surgical spirits can lift some of the paint off your brush handles, but I never want to risk having any bacteria remaining.

I strongly believe that using the same brushes on multiple clients in a row is disgusting, disrespectful of public health and totally unprofessional. You wouldn't want a makeup artist to do it to you or to someone you care about so you shouldn't do it to your clients. Many makeup companies sell inexpensive brush cleaners so there really is no excuse. I've accumulated a lot of brushes over the past few years, so my solution to never running out of clean brushes mightn't be practical for everyone, but I carry multiples of each brush and keep clean ones ready so I know I'll never be stuck. In my brush belt alone, I carry roughly five of each brush, while I also carry an extra brush bag in case I need them. These spare brushes always come in handy for fashion shows and large wedding parties. The majority of the brushes I use are, individually, quite cheap and I'm definitely not married to any one brand for brushes. The longer you work in the industry, the more you'll notice that you can accidentally lose brushes or they might fall out of your kit bag on set. If that brush cost you €60 you'll be devastated, but if it cost you €3, you won't mind quite as much. I usually order directly from large makeup brush manufacturers which usually tend to be both good value as well as great quality.

One final point I'll add on the topic of brush hygiene is that I would never recommend putting your used, dirty brushes back into your brush belt along with your clean unused brushes. The bacteria from the dirty ones will spread on to your other brushes as well as all over your belt, so keep them separate. I carry nappy bags (yes, pound shop nappy bags, usually used for nappies) and I put my used brushes into them when I'm finished so that they're kept separate at all times. Problem solved.

Please think about your client before putting their health as well as your reputation at risk.

Keeping brushes out of creams

Never put your brush into any cream product. This includes lipsticks, cream blushers, cream foundations, concealers and any other liquids. Bacteria thrives in these products, so to prevent nasties from moving in, I always take the product out with a spatula or the end of my sanitised brush and either put some on a palette or onto the back of my sanitised hand. Just think – if you have a beautiful lipstick palette and each time you use it, you put your brush directly back onto the product you're constantly leaving bacteria behind. Fast forward 100 clients and that's a monstrous number of bacteria now living on your once beautiful lipstick. Keep your brushes out.

Note that this doesn't apply to powder products as bacteria doesn't survive on dry surfaces, so there's no need to ruin your eyeshadows and blushers by scraping off product.

Mascara wands

I'm not a fan of using the same mascara wand on numerous clients – even the thought of it upsets my stomach. A reused mascara wand will transform into a playground for bacteria and will start to smell bad very quickly. Disposable mascara wands are very cheap: twice a year I place a large order online and, most recently, I got 1,000 wands for €30 with free shipping. The only time I ever use the mascara wand that comes with the product on a client is when it's nearly empty. I'll use it and then give the mascara to that client to keep as I won't be using it again. They'll get a few more uses out of it and will be delighted with the freebie! One final point: don't ever double-dip the same disposable mascara wand back into the product. This completely defeats the whole purpose of using one so always remember: **one wand per use.** If you need to apply more, bin the used one and get a new wand.

Keeping your kit clean the easy way

The other day I took my entire kit apart, cleaned everything and then put it back together again. It was a blissful, three-hour process (and no, I'm not joking, it did take that long). Your kit will cost you a lot of money over the years so why wouldn't you want it to look it's best? After each client, I quickly wipe down each product that I used before I put it back in my kit. I either do it with a baby wipe or a tissue and it only takes a second. This saves you having to go home, take your kit apart and clean everything, even the products that you didn't use (which is what I used to do). I still like to do that about once a month but by just cleaning what you've used when you're repacking your kit, you can stay on top of it very easily. To some people this might seem unnecessary but it's really important to me. I believe that you should give your best to your clients and there's no sadder sight than a dirty kit.

Hands and breath

It is absolutely vital that you sanitise your hands before you start working on a client. This will get rid of any bacteria and will leave your hands smelling nice and fresh. Hand sanitiser is very cheap, available in most shops and comes in a wide range of scents so take your pick: your clients will thank you for it. Also, be conscious of your breath and use a mint spray just before starting an application.

3.11 BASIC HAIR KIT

Makeup artists are often asked to also do hair on photoshoots. I know what you're thinking: 'But Ciara, that's a totally different job isn't it?'. The quick answer is yes, it is, but sometimes for a shoot, if the company can get a makeup artist to do both, then they'll be saving some money as they won't need to hire a separate hairstylist. I'm not saying this is right but it's just what happens occasionally. You can charge extra for doing hair so a few years ago I learned the basics.

A hair kit doesn't need to be anything too complicated. Below I've included a list of the key products that I carry and use most often:

- Blowdryer.
- Hair straightener.
- Curling wand/tongs.
- Strong-hold hairspray.
- Medium-hold hairspray.
- Hair ties and hair pins/grips.
- Dry shampoo.
- Serum.
- Texturising spray.
- Men's wax.
- Men's wet-look gel.
- Men's styling clay.
- Male grooming bag, including an electric razor, disposable razors and shaving foam.

I carry my hair kit in a small suitcase that has four wheels and weighs very little, so it's easy to bring it along to photoshoots. I keep it in the boot of my car 99 percent of the time, just in case I need it.

3.12 THE THINGS YOU THOUGHT YOU'D NEVER NEED

A lot of people get a great deal of amusement when I list off the random non-makeup pieces of kit that I bring with me on photoshoots. Where some do seem a bit strange, I have needed all of them at one time or another so I'd recommend throwing your eyes over the list below (please try not to laugh):

First-aid kit

Include bandages (plasters) and alcohol swabs. All too often female models will cut their feet on aptly named 'killer heels' while on set, so be a doll and have a bandage at the ready.

A high chair/stool

Doing makeup on a client who's sitting on a low chair is a total nightmare. Not only does it take a lot of the enjoyment out of the whole process as your back will get sore, it can also be uncomfortable for your client. The chair doesn't have to be anything fancy, just a light folding chair that can be kept in the back seat of your chair. It'll be the best €24 you'll ever spend. Often photography studios will have a high chair, but if you're going out to a client's house or are shooting on location, always bring your own.

Tampons

I'll never forget the time when, long ago, I was assisting a very well-known body painter and, just as we were getting started, the model whispered to me that she thought she'd just got her period. She couldn't have possibly been more exposed: all she was wearing was a flesh-coloured thong and two nipple covers. She asked me if I had any tampons – I didn't, so I ran out to the nearest shop and bought some. I've carried some in my kit ever since, in case a similar situation should ever arise.

Safety pins

Makeup artists are, for some reason, expected to carry pretty much everything in their kit. I couldn't tell you how many times I've been asked for safety pins on a shoot – usually it's to pin the clothing to fit the model better. I always have a stash of pins in my set bag just in case.

Hair pins and elastics

Even if you don't do hair, you'll still sometimes be asked for hair pins if they have no hairstylist on set and a model's hair needs to be adjusted slightly. Go to your local salon supply store and get some packs of hair pins, in light as well as dark colours, and some hair elastics. Keep them with your safety pins so you'll always know just where they are in case you need them.

Medication

Now, I'm not talking about hard drugs here, but if you're on a long photoshoot it can be quite common for someone to feel a bit under the weather or have a headache. In my mini first-aid kit, I carry things like painkillers, antihistamines, throat lozenges and tablets for upset stomachs. Always ask if the person has any allergies first.

Hairdressing gown

A gown is handy to have if you're doing makeup for a TV presenter and they're already dressed to go on camera. The last thing you want to do is spill powder all over their clothes, so by having a gown in your kit, you will save yourself any heartache in situations like this.

Disposable head cover

Let me paint you a picture: you've just perfected the most incredible makeup that you have ever done in your entire life and the model is getting changed for the first shot. Unfortunately, the top she's getting into is quite tight around the neck and – without meaning to, of course – she has just smudged your makeup, which now needs about 20 minutes of touch-ups, delaying the whole shoot. Some stylists will bring along a headscarf for the model to put over her face while changing clothes so as to protect both the clothes and the makeup, but not all of them do. I always carry a few disposable head covers in my kit. They are available online.

Basic special-effects kit

Even though you aren't necessarily an SFX artist, you might be asked to do some basic special effects on a photoshoot. Sometimes it can be as simple as adding some sweat gel to a footballer's brow for a sports campaign or adding some dirt to an actor's face. If you have an interest in this area of makeup, a lot of the most talented artists I've ever met in this field are self-taught, so don't be afraid to get stuck in and start teaching yourself. Even if you're not specialising in this area, I'd recommend having a few basic cream colours for blood and bruising, liquid blood, sweat gel, stipple sponges and dirt pigment, as you just never know when you might need them.

STAGE 4:

BE THE BEST YOU CAN BE

Always ask your client if they have any allergies before you start applying makeup. No exceptions.

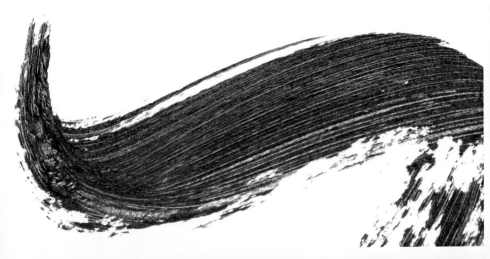

4.1 PERSONAL PRESENTATION

It took me a while to realise that the way I acted in public was how people would see my business. As a sole trader, you are your company 24/7. This is what led me to stop drinking alcohol back in 2012. I didn't want to run into a client while drunk and not in my right mind, waiting on a taxi on the side of the road shovelling chips down my throat. This is not how I wanted people to see me, so I stopped. Alcohol is a funny one because it tricks you into thinking that you're having the time of your life but it's viewed through heavily clouded glasses. What you're seeing in that moment is not what everyone else is seeing, so do be careful. This isn't to say that everyone should stop drinking but it's a good thing to have in the back of your mind that it could negatively affect your business one day.

Your personal presentation covers everything, from your clothes, your hair and how you smell to your makeup, your nails and the way you hold yourself in public. I feel more confident when I'm wearing something nice and am well put-together. Whether I'm on a photoshoot or having a meeting with a potential client, I want to give the same impression: that I'm a professional and that I know what I'm doing.

A note on nails: as a makeup artist, it's important to keep them clean and polished, as dirty nails, with polish from six months ago, that's 66 percent chewed off, doesn't quite appeal to most clients. You will also really notice it if you see an artist doing a demo on TV and they don't have their nails done. The camera could focus right in on your fingers and you want them to look clean and put together, just like the rest of you. I feel so much better when I have a bright coloured, long-lasting polish on my nails. Don't neglect your paws.

Transport

When I started out, for three long years I had to use public transport to get around as I hadn't learned to drive yet. It was an absolute nightmare. If you know how outdated the poor Irish transport system is you'll understand this fully. I would have to leave my house three hours before I had to be anywhere in case my train was delayed or it just didn't show up, which happened more often than it should. I was dragging my kit around in the sun, rain and wind and it was exhausting, not to mention frustrating.

I learned to drive four years ago and have not once taken my car for granted since. The freedom it's given me and the time it saves still amazes me to this day. I would strongly recommend that you get a car if you can as carrying a heavy makeup kit on public transport can be a complete nightmare.

Don't burden your clients with your problems

I've always felt that it's vitally important to show people my best side when I'm working. Sure, we all have issues and go through unpleasant things in our lives, but I'd never want to burden clients with my problems when they've treated themselves to having their makeup done. Imagine if you went to the hairdressers for a treat, a bit of peace and quiet as you've recently just lost your job, and the stylist is telling you, in great detail, about a drunken row she had with her boyfriend last night because she was flirting with his best friend. As a client, you don't need to know this information unless you're a close personal friend.

Yes, of course you can have a real conversation about things like mental health, but only if your client has brought it up first. Over the years, I've learned so much about people and I then use this intuition to casually bring up some of my own struggles to make them feel more relaxed; then, in turn they can also share some of their own battles if they feel like it. This, in the past, has led to some of the most amazing conversations I've ever had. Clients like these ones will usually stay in touch after the appointment because we've connected over something real, something we can both understand and that we totally relate to. We are all human and go through the same things.

Personal style

Most makeup artists tend to wear black clothes because we're usually backstage, behind the scenes and don't want to draw attention to ourselves. I must've missed that memo when I dyed my hair bright orange with a bright yellow streak! As it's a creative industry, artists will usually have their own style and are encouraged to express themselves in their image. Even though I look different, I'll always wear something presentable to a job or to a meeting. My uniform tends to be a black blazer and black top paired with black skinny jeans, converse and some form of ridiculous accessory that is usually found hanging from my ears. While I do have my own style and look unique, I will always present myself professionally to my clients. With that in mind, I've an interesting story to tell you.

A few years ago, I met a woman who wanted to hire a makeup artist to teach a course. A friend recommended I get in touch with this individual, so I did; we set up a meeting and off I went. Before we get down to it, keep in mind that this was before I had any visible tattoos, my hair was my natural colour and long (on both sides of my head) and I applied my makeup very naturally. I wore all black, was polite and presented myself well from the moment I stepped into the building. When I met this person, I shook her hand, said it was lovely to meet her and maintained eye contact (this is important to show that you're confident, professional and not intimidated).

She took a seat behind her desk and I in front of it. Expecting the usual questions, like who have I worked for, my past experience in teaching, etc., instead, I was met with a question of a very different nature. One that I hadn't prepared for. Those five little words fell out of her mouth as naturally as breathing: 'You're a bit weird looking'. Silence. She kept talking, while I planned my response and focused on keeping calm.

Then came another blow as she asked, 'Well, what do you think about that?' I could sense it: she was ready for the verbal abuse that would follow – in fact, she was looking forward to it. Her anticipation was like a loud electrical buzz in the air. I refused to give her what she wanted; instead, I stayed calm. You see, had I flown off the handle and told her to shove her job and her bad manners somewhere unpleasant, I would have been exactly who she thought I was. I would've been unprofessional and unpredictable, but instead I saw this as my opportunity to be the bigger person.

I still remember exactly what I said in reply. I took every scrap of emotion off the table, took a deep breath, and said:

'You have a right to your own opinion and I respect that, but as I work in the fashion industry, most artists tend to have their own style. In fact, in most cases, it's encouraged.'

Short, sweet and well phrased. In my head though, of course, I was thinking about what I'd actually like to say to her. The obscenities I would throw in her face would make small babies cry and old people need a sit down. Instead I felt sorry for her. If that's how she judged others, I wonder how she judges herself.

We finished our meeting, I lied and told her that it was a pleasure to meet her and we both went our separate ways, knowing that we would never see each other again. That was until this encounter must have slipped her mind and she contacted me a few years later for a favour on a project she was working on. I'm sure you can guess what my response was.

So always be professional, be true to yourself and if someone doesn't like you, hold your head high and move on.

4.2 CLIENT ETIQUETTE & DEALING WITH DIFFICULT CLIENTS

How you get along with your clients will affect whether they book you again or not. It's important that you never take them for granted because with so many makeup artists out there, your client won't have to look very far if they want to go to someone else. Here are my top tips for dealing with your clients:

Bookings

- When a client is booking you for an appointment, it's important to make the process as easy as possible. If they contact you via email, make sure you respond to them before the end of the day, being polite, friendly and enthusiastic.
- Make sure that you have their contact number. If they book you a few weeks in advance, text or email them two days beforehand to reconfirm the appointment. This will eliminate the chance of a no-show.

- Make sure they know how much the appointment will cost before it takes place. Makeup applications can cost anything from €5 to €5,000 so don't presume your client will know the cost.
- Before the appointment takes place, ask them what type of makeup looks they like and whether they have any specific reference images of looks that they love. If they do, ask them to email them to you so you can get an idea of their vision. This will help you to be as prepared as possible for the appointment and will prevent any wires from being crossed.

Preparation
- Always be set up and ready to go for your appointment at least ten minutes before it's scheduled to start. If you're late and they're on time, you will look unorganised and unprofessional. You'll also be stressed, making the appointment an unpleasant experience for your client.
- When they arrive, greet the client with a friendly handshake and say how lovely it is to meet them. It's important to set the appointment off on the right tone. A lot of this will depend on your personality type but I always want to make my clients feel as relaxed as possible.

During the appointment
- Know that it's not about you. Your focus for that hour needs to be on your client, so ask them about themselves and get to know a bit about them.
- Your client will most likely give you a list of all of the things she hates about herself but try and get her to see herself in a positive light. I couldn't even take a guess at how many women have

sat in my chair and told me how awful their skin is when it's actually perfect. Our job is to not only make them look their best but, more importantly, to feel their best.

- Before you start applying any product, ask them if they have any allergies. Some people have reactions to certain brands so it's a good habit to get into to always ask beforehand.
- Ask them how their skin usually is as this will help you to figure out what foundation will work best.
- Don't presume that because a client is a certain age that they want a certain makeup look. You could have an older client that wants something bold and dramatic or a teenager who wants something very natural. Presumption can get you in a lot of trouble, so approach every client with an open mind. At the end of the day, if they know what they want, it's your job to give it to them but if they ask for your advice or to surprise them, that's a different approach and you can follow what you think will look the best.
- Throughout the appointment, make sure your client is comfortable, and keep the conversation flowing. Some people can be a bit more difficult than others but try your very best to keep the mood friendly and light. Ask about family, friends, holidays, hobbies: all the classics!
- I always ask a few times throughout the appointment if they're happy so far. This is where having a medium-sized mirror in your kit will come in handy. You want them to feel like they're in control of what the overall look will be like. If they don't see it until the very end, you risk them hating it, so don't be afraid to ask them what they think. The great thing about makeup is that it can easily be wiped off, so don't worry.

Dealing with challenges

- If your client is giving out about someone, such as a friend or a boyfriend, be supportive but don't say anything that you could later regret. If she tells you she wants to break up with her boyfriend because he had an affair but they actually end up getting married, you'll regret telling her what a jerk he is. It's happened quite a few times that a client of mine has been giving out about someone and they aren't aware that I know that person very well – I'll never say anything. It would be so awkward and sometimes it's best to just keep quiet.

- If they want you to change something, don't take it personally and let it ruin the appointment. It's like when you go to the hairdressers: sometimes you just need to brush it a certain way before you feel totally happy with it. Your client will appreciate that you value her opinion and sometimes I'll even give them the makeup brush and let them do exactly what they want. At the end of the day it doesn't affect me and it isn't insulting in any way. I would never do this with a model on a photoshoot as I would be judged heavily on how the makeup looks in the pictures. The model is there to model, not tell the makeup artist what to do, but with a client who is getting her makeup done for a special occasion, once she's happy that's all that matters.

- Remember that your client does her own makeup a certain way every single day of her life, whether it suits her or not. You may have never met her before and have no idea what she usually looks like. If your client has been wearing bright-blue eyeliner on her lower lashline since Lionel Richie was in the charts, it's unfair for you to tell her that you think it makes her look awful. Even if it does, there are better ways to go about bringing up the topic. A lot of people get stuck in a makeup habit, not necessarily because they like it that way but because they don't know how else to do it. If she wears blue liner (or similar), in a roundabout way ask her what she likes about it and if she says she loves how it looks, don't be cruel and tell her it ages her 20 years. Makeup is a form of personal expression and while there may be certain guidelines, there are no rules. If your client wants a change, this is where you can recommend other colours and textures that would look amazing on her. But if she likes the way she looks, you don't have the right to try and change her.

Wrapping up

- At the end of the appointment, get her to take a good look in the mirror and ask if she'd like more or less of anything. It's always easier to apply a little less to begin with and add a bit more if needed, instead of the other way around. Keep in mind that you'll most likely be using a lot of products that she's never tried before so it might take her a few minutes to get used to her new look. Again, it's just makeup, so if she's not happy, tone down any areas that she's not so keen on.
- Once she's happy, and has paid, tell her you hope she has a great day and you hope to see her again soon.

Dealing with difficult clients

I've always felt that I have such a responsibility to my clients. Regardless of who they are or where they come from, whether they're a celebrity or my next-door neighbour, I want to make them feel as amazing as I possibly can. One of my favourite parts of this job is the fact that I get to meet and hang out with different people each and every day. This isn't to say that some clients won't leave you feeling awful. I'll be very honest and say that over the past few years, I've had a couple of clients who have left me sitting in my car after our appointment in tears, feeling like the worst makeup artist in the whole world. It would shake my confidence for a few days, make me question myself as well as occasionally making me feel like I'm in the wrong profession.

One of the most difficult parts of being a makeup artist is that you are dealing with people who can be unhappy with how they look to begin with. A lot of the work I do with clients borders on a counselling session as well as a beauty experience. When you're working that closely with people, how they feel about themselves will be visible in the way they sit, the way they speak and whether they can make eye contact with you or not. People can feel very stripped back and bare when they have no makeup on, so it's important to pick up on any insecurities they may have. Usually they'll list off all of the things that they hate about themselves so you need to try and counteract that. If a client says that she has awful skin but I can see that her skin is actually perfect, I'll tell her that. In fact, I'll insist that she is seeing things differently to how they really are. We have a responsibility to try and build up our clients' self-confidence whenever we can.

The wisdom I'm about to share with you is important to remember daily. Actually, I demand you write it down somewhere you will regularly see it, because this is major.

Are you ready? Here goes:

Some people just cannot be pleased.

Just in case it didn't quite sink in, I'm going to say it one
more time:

SOME PEOPLE JUST CANNOT BE PLEASED.

You can do your very best work, do every single thing they ask, use every
makeup trick you've ever learned, use your new highlighter that cost
you more than your car insurance and they just still won't be happy.
It's truly not your fault. You followed what your client said she wanted
down to the last brush stroke, you showed her a mirror throughout the
process to make sure she was happy so far, which she was, but at the
end, she apparently still didn't like it. You can feel the physical weight
of that appointment on your shoulders as you put your makeup kit into
the boot of your car, as you carefully reverse out of her driveway and
disappear towards the roundabout. You can feel it for the next week –
like the feeling when you know you're about to get sick but it hasn't
happened just yet.

Then it arrives: an email. She wasn't happy. She didn't like the look
you created so she would like her wedding booking deposit refunded as
she is going to go with another makeup artist for her big day. You feel
like you've been kicked in the stomach and the wind has been well and
truly knocked out of your sails. As you scan down through the email, you
feel your face getting red, your body getting warmer and the urge to cry

creeps up inside you.

In the past, when this has happened to me, I've been with my boyfriend. He can tell by my sudden silence that something is wrong. He wonders where my smile has gone and whether I'm going to finish that rude joke I was in the middle of telling. He looks over my shoulder and quickly understands. He'll always say the right thing, and his words are worth repeating so you can remember them for when you need them:

- 'Don't mind her. You know you did exactly what she said she wanted!'
- 'Wasn't that the Client you said was a nightmare?'
- 'Don't worry about it, she would be a disaster on her Wedding Day. You're lucky that you don't have to work with her again.'
- 'Just think of all of the amazing experiences you've had with other clients – the ones who send you cards and flowers.'
- 'Sometimes it's just not worth it. You know that some people just can't be pleased, right?'

And I know he's right. I believe every single word and know in my gut that he's telling the truth, but there's still a hint of doubt, and that doubt can thrive. I temporarily let this client hurt my feelings. But in the end I have to remember that I wholeheartedly do everything in my power to please my clients, and if they just can't be pleased then that isn't a reflection on me. It's important to always focus on the positive experiences you've had, and try to forget the bad ones. At the end of the day, we work with makeup and brushes, not scalpels, gauze and stitches.

4.3 ETIQUETTE ON SET & WORKING TO A BRIEF

It's important to understand how you should behave whilst on a photoshoot. This can vary, depending on the type of job.

Fashion editorial
These shoots can sometimes be quite relaxed but don't take that as a given as I've also been on some very stressful ones. Editorials tend to be made up on eight to ten different looks so it's important to be conscious of time throughout the day. While doing touch-ups, try to be as quick as possible and make sure that the makeup looks as good in the first shot as it does eight hours later in the final frame. You never know what shot could end up on the magazine cover so be extra vigilant. Usually you'll have one hour to do the makeup, it won't necessarily be said but that's the general assumption. If you have less time than that, you will be told. While you need to be careful in terms of timing, do make sure that if you need a few extra minutes to get the look just right, let the photographer and stylist know. The photographer usually appreciates it as whatever you do will save them some time when it comes to editing.

Commercial shoot
These types of jobs can be a bit more formal because as well as the crew, the client will sometimes come along on the day as well. If it's for a business like a bank or an insurance company, the vibe might be a bit more formal so mould yourself to suit your surroundings.

Photoshoot dos and don'ts

Don't:

Show up hungover. It's unprofessional and you risk not being booked by that client again because of it.

Arrive late. As I've mentioned already, being exactly on time is, to me, the same as being late. Be at least 10 to 15 minutes early, as this shows that you're reliable and take what you do seriously.

Take too long doing the makeup. What this means can vary a lot depending on the type of look you're creating and also on how much time the hairstylist will need. Before you start, ask the photographer or stylist what time they'd like to start shooting and work around that. Don't waste time chatting; instead, when you arrive at the job, get set up right away and be ready to go. Take every spare minute you possibly can to perfect the makeup and be considerate of what the hairstylist needs to do also. It ain't just about you babe!

Be high-maintenance. It's important that while on a long shoot, the crew all get along and everyone is pleasant to be around for long periods of time. Some of the best makeup artists won't get booked for certain jobs because they're really high maintenance, so try to be easy to get along with and a pleasure to be around. Don't be negative about the client, as that will create an uncomfortable atmosphere on set. Remember, just because you work for them doesn't mean you have to like them.

Talk too much. You need to learn to read your surroundings and adapt to them while on photoshoots. If a job is really stressful, everyone's working very hard to get the looks done and if you're being distracting by talking excessively and not paying attention to what you're supposed to be doing, you're not making the situation any better.

Get in the way. While us makeup artists love touching up the makeup we've done, it's important to only do what you need to and not do it simply for the sake of it. On some shoots, our role is vital and on others it's not as important so sometimes you just need to hang back and wait until you're asked for.

Do:
Be nice to everyone. There can be a lot of people on set and it's important that you're nice to them all. I always say that you never know who you're working with or who someone may go on to be in the future, so always be friendly. I'll never forget the few who were rude to me when I was assisting, so do be careful. Some people like to hold a grudge.

Keep your spirits up. Some jobs can go on for an absurd amount of time, so keep yourself in a good mood and be aware of anyone who may need a giggle to get them through the last few looks. On some jobs, a sense of humour will go a really long way.

Working with models and celebrities

Models and makeup artists usually have a close bond because we work so closely with each other. I always feel that I have a responsibility to make sure that the model is looked after on set as they can be as young as 15 and need occasionally minding to a certain extent. It can be easy to forget that the model is a person in their own right, and when they're being treated badly or being talked about like they're not there, that's unfair. When a new model starts out, they will be nervous and usually quite awkward as they've had no industry experience or training. Over time they will improve, learn their angles and gain more confidence in their abilities.

The majority of the models I've worked with are lovely and I really do care about them. Be aware of their needs while on set and, if they're cold between shots, offer a blanket or your coat. Offer to get them a warm drink or a bottle of water. Little things like these will make a big difference. Some clients will want to work the model to the bone as they paid to use her for the day, but make sure that she gets something to eat and is OK. At the end of the day she will go home and tell her friends and family about the shoot and you want her to have had a good experience to remember, not a bad one.

It's also good manners to ask the model if they would like you to remove their makeup at the end of the shoot before they go home. Particularly if the makeup is quite dramatic, it's a nice touch for them to sit down and you can do a proper cleanse and get them back to the same way that they were when they arrived that morning. I would never do something to a model that I wouldn't do to myself: for example, if I wouldn't put that bright purple eyeshadow on myself because it stains the skin for about a week, don't use it on a model either. She could have a casting for a big beauty campaign the next day and if you can't remove a product fully, she mightn't get the campaign job and her agent might want to have some serious words with you.

Not all models will be pleasant to work with; be nice to them regardless of how rude they are. Sometimes a model can have a big ego and think that they're better than everyone else on set. This kind of ego often stems from a place that is sad and scared, so remember that people are not always who they appear to be. Sometimes you will need to humour these types of models and if they are trying to impress you with some of their recent work, give them what they want and just act impressed.

When working with celebrities you need to be careful as it can usually go one of two ways: either they are incredibly normal, chatty and an absolute pleasure to be around, or they're a self-involved nightmare and won't even look you in the eyes. When this happens, just stay quiet, let them be how they want to be and just get the makeup over with. Don't take it personally: it's just the way they are.

Regardless of the celebrity's attitude, don't take any behind-the-scenes pictures unless you're told it's ok. You need to respect their privacy and be aware that they have a public persona that they need to maintain. Though you might love to get your picture taken with this person, if it doesn't feel right, don't ask. It's also a good idea to do your research before meeting the celebrity so you will have something to talk about, should they feel like a chat.

Working to a brief

As I mentioned in section 2.1, a brief is the direction you're given from the stylist, photographer and/or client, which details the type of makeup look they want you to create. How specific this is can range from directing you down to the very last detail to being very vague indeed. You will sometimes be given the inspiration behind the shoot and then asked to put an idea together. It's important to always consider that makeup is one of many parts that has to fit together. If it doesn't fit, it could ruin everything. Here's an example:

Imagine that you're booked to work on a shoot for a natural skincare company. The company's ethos is based on the power of natural beauty. The styling is soft and beautiful and the garments look like the sky the morning after a heavy rainstorm. The hair is kept natural to highlight the model's angelic features. So, how would you imagine the makeup should look? I'll give you two options below –don't put your hand up until you're sure you've got the right answer:

A) Dramatic, feathered eyelashes, foundation four shades darker than the model's skin-tone because you prefer a more sallow tone, harsh eyebrows with a bold white shimmer highlight under the browbone, finished off with an overdrawn purple matte lip.

Or

B) Soft, barely-there makeup, like the model has just had the best night's sleep of her whole life. She looks refreshed, renewed and light as a feather. Her features are subtly highlighted with creams and her skin lightly patted with a water-based foundation to give a beautiful sheen.

If you answered A, I think you need to go back to page 1, but if you answered B, you're correct! Gold stars all around.

I'll give you one other example. Say you're working on a commercial job for an insurance company. The commercial is focusing on a new service the company are offering which includes a free, six-month gym membership with every premium. Your job is to make up a male model to look like he's working hard in the gym. Do you:

A) Make sure his skin is completely flawless and matted down with a touch of glitter highlight.

Or

B) Apply some sweat gel to his face, neck and arms, and make his hair look a bit dishevelled and sweaty?

If you answered B, you are correct! If you answered A, I'm not mad, just disappointed.

4.4 ORGANISATION

If you ensure that you're organised from the very beginning of your career, you will be saving yourself the hassle of having to break bad habits. This is an instance where you can be the best artist in the world but if you aren't where you're supposed to be when you're supposed to be there, you'll really struggle. I've already drummed into you the importance of catering for a worst-case scenario, always being ready and giving every client a good impression of you even before you've met, so you know I'm slightly obsessive about all this. Here are my top tips for staying organised:

Label your emails

In my Gmail account, I have a range of different folders so I can keep relevant emails together. I have a section for 'work bookings', 'makeup companies', 'weddings', 'misc.', etc. This means that if I was looking for an old email from MAC Cosmetics Head Office, or I need to reconfirm wedding details for my diary, I'll know where to find them.

Don't delete any emails

Even if an email doesn't seem relevant right now, you might need it in the future, so keep it stored away just in case.

Only keep emails in your inbox that still need your attention

As you're all set up now with your new folders, you don't need 132,456,294 emails in your inbox: once you've tended to them, file them away. A messy inbox gives me anxiety – it would make me feel like I still have a lot of work to do. Once I've dealt with an email, I file it away and mentally tick it off a list. There's such a feeling of satisfaction when you've gone through all your emails, filed them all away and your inbox is empty! (You know you're getting a little bit older when you start saying things like that).

Use a diary

A lot of people will use the calendar on their phones for filling in booking information, but I personally like to have a physical diary as well. I get one each year that has a hard cover and gives you a full page per day so you have plenty of room to make any relevant notes. I also have it with me at all times, no exceptions. I do also fill in the calendar on my phone but I just couldn't live without my diary.

Have all of the information

Don't be the type of makeup artist that shows up to the wrong studio for a shoot because they forgot to write down where they were supposed to go. It's an avoidable mistake and would be incredibly embarrassing. Always make sure you've taken down the time, location address and any relevant phone numbers in case you get lost on the day.

Wedding bookings

This is an area that you need to take very seriously. Whether you're a believer in weddings or not, the bride will want her day to be perfect and it won't be perfect if you got the date wrong and don't show up. It's important, particularly when dealing with brides, that you are very clear and organised at all times when communicating with them. You don't want them to doubt your reliability, so check the date and then double check again just in case. Once you take a wedding booking and have received a deposit, I beg you not to cancel on them two weeks before their big day because you were offered a 'better job'. If you have taken money then you have a responsibility to hold up your end of the bargain. You don't want to be known as someone who can't be trusted and believe me, it will get around that you cancelled, because people in this industry love to talk. If you don't want to do weddings, don't do them. Simple. But don't potentially ruin an important day in someone's life because your friend asked you to do her makeup instead. On a final note, don't be the type of makeup artist who puts a post out on their Facebook asking next week's bridal client to get in touch because they can't remember who they are and don't have their contact details.

Always have credit on your phone

The stress of not being able to find a shoot location will be made a hundred times worse if you go to call the stylist only to find that you have no credit in your phone. Signing up to a billpay phone will prevent this from ever happening.

Always prep your kit the night beforehand

The night before a shoot or appointment, make sure you have packed everything you need, have your clean brushes ready to go and double check that you have everything you could possibly need in your worst-case scenario. You could be told that you'll only be doing makeup on one male model, but then when you arrive, find the brief has changed and now you have three female models as well. It doesn't matter that the brief has changed – you should have brought everything just in case. So never be left stuck, cater for all eventualities and don't get caught out.

4.5 BRIDAL MAKEUP

The Bridal business is a huge industry with many makeup artists dedicating themselves purely to looking after brides on their special day. Weddings can be wonderful experiences but it's important to remember that they can be very hard work over a long day, especially if you have to drive a few hours to the location. This needs to be taken into account when you're putting together a bridal quote. The wedding industry is a very lucrative one but it's important to remember that it can also be very tedious when dealing with people on such a stressful day. Below are my top tips when dealing with brides:

Bookings
- Get back to their first enquiry email within 24 hours.

This gives a good first impression that you care about your clients and sets things off on the right tone.

- From the second your bride contacts you, be professional, well organised and friendly, including any email interactions. It's important that they know they'll be in good hands should they book you for their big day.

Quotes and payments

- In terms of pricing, bridal makeup can vary hugely. Each wedding will have a different rate, as it should vary depending on how many people are in the bridal party and how far you need to travel. Before you can put together a quote, ask the bride where the wedding will be, what time the ceremony begins and how many people will be getting their makeup done on the day.

- Your fee will also depend on your experience level. Some people offer wedding packages, but personally, I charge per person, with a set price for trials and travel expenses. A trial should be slightly cheaper than the cost of the makeup on the day and I personally charge an hourly rate for the time spent travelling to the location, there and back. If you have to drive for two hours or more, I would recommend staying in a nearby hotel the night beforehand. Weddings can be exhausting and if you have to drive for two hours, do makeup for eight people and then drive two hours to get back home, you'll risk crashing on the way home. If you need to stay in the area the night beforehand, include the price of a hotel room in your quote – the client will need to cover this expense.

- Always ask for a booking deposit. No exceptions. I charge a

50 percent booking deposit that is non-refundable and I will only hold the date of the wedding once the payment has shown up in my account.

- Always provide a receipt for the deposit and email it as a PDF to your bride.

- To make up a receipt, the easiest way would be to download a receipt template online and adapt it to show your details. Include a receipt number, the date and the amount paid and make a note down the bottom saying that deposits are non-refundable. Also keep a document for your own records of all the receipts that have been sent out, plus their corresponding numbers.

- Always be very clear about money. Make sure that there is no confusion about how much deposit has been paid, how much is outstanding and when it needs to be paid. Money and confusion don't marry very well ('lil wedding pun for you there), so always be clear.

- The remaining balance after the deposit has been paid should be paid before the day of the wedding, or on the morning as soon as you arrive. I've had a few nightmarish situations where the bride has forgotten to get money out to pay me and the hairstylist and a row breaks out between herself and her Dad, as each blames the other for the mistake. It puts such a dampener on the day. Explain before the day of the wedding that sometimes it's better to get any outstanding payments out of the way beforehand so the bride doesn't have to worry about paying anyone on the day.

Trials

- A trial should be done at least a few weeks before the wedding.
- Make sure you get an idea of what type of makeup look the bride has in mind before the trial. Ask her how she usually

wears her makeup, what her favourite products are, how she finds her skin and ask her to send you some reference pictures of the type of makeup she would like for her wedding day. This will give you a general idea of whether she likes a natural look or something a bit more dramatic.

- Give around two hours for a trial.
- I always see a trial as a way of getting to know the bride as a person, as well as figuring out what type of makeup she likes. The last thing you want is to be rushing through the trial as you have another booking straight afterwards, so give yourself plenty of time and don't rush.
- I give my bride a mirror so she can see the look coming together as we go through each step.
- Makeup is such a personal thing and we all do it very differently so I usually apply the foundation, show her and see if she would like me to apply more or less and then once she's happy, I'll move on to the next step. This will prevent her seeing the makeup at the very end and hating every last bit of it. By giving her the mirror you can make sure that she is happy with the look you are creating throughout.
- Never be afraid to take it off and do it again. If you put on a lip colour and she isn't 100 percent happy about it, take it off and try something different. A trial is an opportunity to find a makeup look that works for your bride; sometimes that may take a bit of trial and error.
- Regardless of what you do, it's possible she still won't be happy. This isn't an attack on your skill set, it's just the way it goes sometimes so don't worry about it too much. (Remember our mantra, 'some people just cannot be pleased'.)
- She might say that she wants something 'a bit different', but

in my experience, 95 percent of the time, she doesn't. A wedding day is not the time to be experimenting with different makeup looks so just make sure that she looks like the best version of herself instead of transforming her into an entirely different person.

- Sometimes the look a bride wants isn't actually the look she wants. This is very common. A bride will send me reference pictures of a specific look, for example, a 1950's flicked black eyeliner and a red lip. You have a trial and create the most perfect look and she loves it: she can't stop staring at herself in the mirror and she leaves delighted. Then the next day you get a phone call or an email saying that she wasn't actually happy with it: she never usually wears black eyeliner and red lipstick, and she just didn't feel like herself. Now, you didn't do anything wrong, you actually did everything right. You can just have a second trial and then create a makeup look that is more along the lines of what she usually wears.

- When you get the bride's look right, take a few pictures from different angles and make some notes on the products you used. Then if your trial is successful (and you don't get a concerned call or an email the next day like the story above), you'll know exactly what to do on her wedding day.

- When the look is planned, I recommend that the bride gets a few key products to have with her to touch up her makeup throughout the day. I usually recommend a lipstick, lip gloss (if desired) and a face powder as her skin will get shiny throughout the day. If you have used a good foundation, primed the eyes before applying the eyeshadow and have used waterproof mascara, she shouldn't need to touch up any other area of her makeup.

On the day

- Be a source of calm energy. In my time, I have defused many a crisis situation on the morning of a wedding without the bride knowing. A lot of people will come to the bride with silly things that she doesn't need to be worrying about, so help wherever possible and 'protect' her from stress whenever possible. Stay on top of what's going on and direct any confusion about flowers, guests, etc. to the bridesmaids and not the bride.

- Put on a happy face. On the morning of a wedding, when tensions are high, coping levels are low, family politics are on display and the appetite for Champagne is unquenchable, sometimes your people skills will be more vital than your makeup skills. If you know some of the bridal party are really stressed, do try to lighten the mood and change the subject of conversation, where necessary, to calm them down a bit. It's important as well to gauge when a crisis is about to rear its ugly head so keep your ears open and plan ahead.

- Music can lighten the mood. Playing some music in the background helps to fill any silences and create a nice atmosphere. Sometimes the bridesmaids will make a specific playlist, but if not, offer up your phone with some 80's and 90's pop on it – you just can't go wrong with a bit of cheese!

- I've worked with some truly wonderful brides, including some that I still keep in touch with, so don't fall into the mindset that all brides are the same – they're not.

4.6 LONDON FASHION WEEK & SHOWS

One of the things that I was determined to do ever since I became a makeup artist was to work at London Fashion Week. I've always been so in love with seeing the makeup looks that are created for each show and how the looks tie in with each designer's new collection, and I always wondered what it would be like to be backstage. In 2016, after a lot of work, I finally got there.

On my way there, though, I wished there was some type of list to help makeup artists get onto their desired path. Say, if you wanted to work for British Vogue, you simply have to work your butt off for ten years, make all the right contacts, don't take no for an answer, hustle to meet the stylists that work for the magazine and then on the eighth day of the seventh month you will reach your destination in the form of an editorial shoot for, you guessed it, British Vogue. Maybe that's unwittingly what I was trying to do when I started writing this book. There have been so many times over the past few years when I just wished I had someone to ask for advice to help me find my way, and I never want you to feel that way. That's why I've been squeezing every last bit of makeup industry knowledge I have onto these pages.

Back to Fashion Week. I can't speak for how other people get their places backstage, so instead I'll just tell you how I got myself there. In my experience, the main ways to get backstage are to:

- Be on the events team for a makeup brand. Most brands have some kind of pro team that represents the company at events. If the brand you work for are sponsoring a Fashion Week show and you're on this team, you should hopefully be booked to work backstage.

- Work with an established makeup artist who keys a lot of shows. A key artist is the one that the rest of the team work under who is booked to design and execute the makeup look. If you have assisted a well-known makeup artist and have a good working relationship with them, then they will hopefully book you to be on their makeup team for Fashion Week. If a brand is sponsoring the show and is using their own pro team, the key artist might put you forward to work with them.

- Get in touch with the agencies that represent well-known makeup artists. Agencies are an integral part of the whole process. If a makeup artist they represent is doing a number of shows, they will organise a lot of the logistics for the teams so it's vital that you're on their radar. Look up some of the big international artists and contact their agents, introducing yourself. Send over examples of your work, give a brief bio and say that you will be in London for Fashion Week if they need you. Contact them about eight weeks before the show starts in your desired city, then follow up every week in the month leading up to the start of Fashion Week. You really need to fight for your place on these teams and, as a freelance artist, it really isn't an easy process.

How I got to work at London Fashion Week was a true testament to how I never give up when I really want something. For the first three years of my freelance career, I worked on building up a good working relationship with one of the biggest makeup brands in the world, MAC Cosmetics. Their UK Head Office is based in London so every time I went over, I would ask if they could meet me for a coffee and see my updated portfolio. Also, whenever they were over in Dublin I would hound them to meet with me. I met with them twice a year for three years before anything came of it. Each time we met, I would sell myself by telling them all of my recent jobs, who I've been working with, where my work was being published and really show off how hard I've been working on my portfolio. I also always brought up the topic of whether they would hire a freelance makeup artist to work on one of their team's backstage for London Fashion Week and each time I was told no. They said that the only freelance artists they hire are the assistants of the key artist – unfortunately no others.

After each meeting, I would send a follow-up email saying how lovely it was to see them again and that I would stay in touch. Fast forward to November 2015 when I set up a meeting while they were over in Dublin for a big event. Again, I got dolled up, put my game face on and brought my updated makeup portfolio, which was filled with brand-new prints. As they flicked through my portfolio, I could tell that something had changed. They were really excited to see my new work and were impressed with everything that I'd been doing. And then the most shocking thing happened. Are you ready for this? Because I know I wasn't! They asked me if I would be interested in working with them at London Fashion Week next season, which was in February 2016. I couldn't believe it. I hadn't had the chance to bring up the topic yet and they just offered it on the table like it was the most natural thing. I acted cool – 'Yeah sure, why not' – but inside, I was singing 'I'm so excited' by the Pointer Sisters.

So, in February 2016, I flew over and I got to work on the Paul Smith Autumn-Winter 16 show. It was such an amazing experience, and I learned that persistence pays off. While there really is no direct route to get to the job you want, and a lot of it comes down to who you know and being in the right place at the right time, so much can be said for pushing yourself every day, never giving up and never taking 'no' for an answer.

I have one other Fashion Week story, but this one doesn't end so well.

In fact, it doesn't end well at all. After AW16, I decided that I would try to get on a team for Spring-Summer 17, which was still a few months away. I made a list of the key artists who were heading a lot of the shows, found out who their agents were and got in touch. I kept following up with them weekly as the shows got closer and I couldn't believe it, but I got confirmed to work on four shows at London Fashion Week SS17 with Andrew Gallimore, who is one of my favourite makeup artists of all time. I was elated and felt that all of my work up to now was leading to this moment.

My flights and accommodation were booked and paid for and I was leaving in two days' time. I had recently had surgery on my throat so I had a check-up appointment with my surgeon. The average waiting time was three hours to see him so I sat in a stuffy overcrowded waiting room that was grim as hell and read the latest issue of Vogue. While I was waiting, my phone went off and I saw that I had an email from Andrew's agent. He said unfortunately I had been cancelled on all four shows, as Andrew now had a different schedule for Fashion Week, so I wasn't needed.

I would go so far as to say that that was one of the most heartbreaking moments of my entire life, to date. I finally felt like I was getting somewhere and then all of a sudden, I was back crawling on the ground again, barely scraping by. I wanted to cry but I couldn't, so I held it together until I was called by the doctor, got the all-clear and quickly made my way to my car.

Thirty minutes later I pulled up outside my house, opened the front door, walked straight through to the kitchen, unlocked the back door and went out to the garden. I let myself fall on the grass and finally gave myself permission to cry. I was totally and utterly devastated. My boyfriend, Paul, knew to give me some space and that I would be fine once I just got all of the sadness out. I felt like a failure, like I had somehow done something wrong, even though it had nothing to do with me. After 35 minutes of crying my heart out until I had nothing left, I picked myself up off the grass, brushed the fluffy dandelion seeds off my knees and heavily stepped back into the house. Paul looked at me, concerned, but I told him that I was OK now. The funny thing was I didn't look OK, as I had been crying for half an hour, had grass stains all over my clothes and had a scar across my neck that still hadn't quite healed yet.

Before you ask, yes, I did still go to London. I made the most of my time there and set up a photoshoot, as well as a few meetings with PR companies. Things can often change at the last minute in this industry for all types of reasons, so you need to know that until you are there backstage, there is always a chance that you could be cancelled and someone else will be standing there, instead, in your place. The journey can be hard but no one ever said that it would be easy.

Fashion shows

If you get asked to do makeup for a fashion show, make sure you get all of the information before you send over a quote. They can be a lot of work, as you could have up to 30 models for makeup so you will need to bring other artists to work alongside you. Some fashion shows can be in aid of charities – note that you wouldn't usually be paid for these.

If the show start time is 6pm, your calltime could be as early as 9am. If there are a lot of models and the catwalk routine is complicated, they will need to do rehearsals and a full run-through before you get the models for makeup. Also consider that the hair team will need enough time to create their look and, finally, the models will need to be styled and dressed for the show. Fashion shows can be great fun but are also quite stressful – you'll need to be organised.

The show will usually have a general theme, such as spring-summer or autumn-winter wear. The makeup will need to tie in with the rest of each look, so make sure you get a brief and take into account what the hair will be like. Sometimes, if the hair is a bit on the wild side, it's a good idea to keep the makeup more muted to balance it out, or vice versa. You will also need to consider your timing because if you have a lot of models to work on, you can't spend one hour with each one. The look will need to be something that all of the artists on your team can achieve in a small amount of time.

You'll also need to take into account the fact that the makeup team, which will all be replicating the look you show them, will need to use products the same as or similar to yours. If you're doing a specific lip shade, make sure all the artists have either the full lipstick or make up sample pots with the shade in it to share around.

Once the rehearsals and hair and makeup are complete, the models will be dressed and lined up ready to go. Here you can do final makeup checks, which will usually involve some face powder and topping up the lip. Also apply some body makeup and highlighter to the legs if needed. When the show starts, stay out of the way backstage as the models will need to be changed from one outfit to the next very quickly and you don't want to delay the process.

STAGE 5:

RATES, AGENCIES & EXPERIENCE

Because if you don't value what you do, no one else will.

5.1 TYPES OF WORK AVAILABLE & WHAT YOU SHOULD CHARGE

The work of a makeup artist can vary hugely, but most people think that we either only work on a makeup counter or do occasion makeup for women. Makeup artists are responsible for doing so much more. For every magazine cover, every billboard, every TV show and every ad for a new type of toothpaste, a makeup artist has worked on that shoot. And don't think that just because they have a male model or celebrity on the cover that they didn't have a makeup artist working on them, because I guarantee you that they did.

Below is a list of the main areas of work and general pay rates for each. Note that these rates are a guide, and will obviously go up or down depending on your level of experience and expertise. It's important to never charge too little, as it's always better to quote too high and then you have the chance to bring the price down a little if needs be. By charging too little to begin with, you risk never being able to charge a client the full rate, so do be careful.

Fashion editorials
Unpaid to €250+ per day
Having your work published in a magazine is a great way to get your name out there. I'll be very honest with you: fashion can be a very tricky area to try and make any kind of money in. A lot of magazines will try to get away with paying everyone else on the team (the photographer, model and stylist) but unfortunately find there is 'no budget' to pay for hair and makeup. I'm not quite sure who came up with this concept but the idea that hair and makeup has no monetary value blows my mind. Trust me, hair and makeup have the power to either make or break a

shoot, so it is without a doubt worth investing in someone who actually knows what they're doing. I've seen so many shoots that would've been amazing had they just got an experienced artist instead of using someone with little-to-no experience who would do it for free.

Working on photoshoots is completely different to working on, say, a makeup counter. On photoshoots, you need to have a good understanding of lighting, shadows and how different looks photograph. Every shoot will be different and there are many things to take into account, like if you're shooting outdoors in cool weather, you will need to put body makeup on the model so her skin doesn't look cold and blue. But between each outfit change, you will need to clean off this makeup so she can get changed into the next look without risking getting makeup all over the clothes. Once dressed, you will most likely have to repeat the process again. Also consider the nails and if they need painting.

Some magazines may ask you to work for credit. This means that you can contact a makeup brand, ask them to sponsor you for the shoot and then, if you get the magazine to print 'Makeup by Ciara Allen using [makeup brand]', the brand will give you payment or a certain number of products for being mentioned. This can be great for building up your kit, as some brands will offer 10–12 products of your choice per shoot, but over the years when you've done quite a few of them, the appeal isn't quite as strong. Of course, it's great having your work published in magazines, but obviously the work we do is valuable and like every other member of the team on a photoshoot, we deserved to be paid for our time and hard work. My advice would be do the shoot if it benefits you, if you're free and if it's with a team that you really like. If so, you'll get some great images for your portfolio and it's definitely worth doing. I personally wouldn't do it if I thought the shots or the team wouldn't do my work any justice but this is all down to personal choice and experience. You can read more about what it means to work for credit in section 5.4.

Brand advertorials
Up to €500 per day

As the name indicates, an advertorial is an editorial-style photoshoot that is led by advertising a certain brand or product. That brand would pay a magazine to publish the shoot as it's another way to advertise their products to a larger audience. The rate you should charge for these is higher because brands have a larger budget and hair and makeup will always get paid a proper commercial day rate. No exceptions.

Commercial photoshoot
Up to €500 per day

This type of shoot relates to any type of advertising job for a company or brand. Think of an advertisement for a bank, a sportswear company featuring a new type of running shoe, or a college – the list is endless. The looks are generally simple enough as most ads recreate real-life scenarios, but there are always exceptions.

Lookbook photoshoot
€150–500+

A lookbook is a photoshoot showcasing a designer's latest collection. It would usually focus on a range of looks from either their Spring-Summer or their Autumn-Winter collection. Day rates vary according to how established the designer/brand is, and are usually negotiable.

Makeup lessons
Around €150 for a two-hour session

Makeup lessons are great for people who want to learn, from a professional artist, in the comfort of their own home, how to do their own makeup. The rate will vary depending on how long a lesson your client wants, what they want to learn and whether they would want multiple sessions or a one-off.

Private clients
Between €50-€120 per person

This is an area that will vary, depending on what experience you have in the industry. Always take into account how much travelling you will have to do to get to your clients house and make sure that travel time is covered in your rate.

Weddings
Rates vary depending on experience

Weddings are a tricky one, as some people might charge €20 per person, while others will charge €200. Keep your level of experience in mind when setting your prices. For a bridal trial, I recommend that you charge slightly less than your fee on the day, so if you will charge €80 per person on the day of the wedding, maybe charge somewhere between €50–70 for the trial. For weddings, you will also need to incorporate your time spent travelling in your quote as well as getting a 50 percent deposit to secure the booking.

5.2 UNPAID WORK: GOOD EXPERIENCE OR EXPLOITATION?

It's inevitable that when you first start out, you will do a lot of unpaid work to build up contacts and experience. This is fine for a certain amount of time, but you won't be able to financially survive like that forever. On some unpaid jobs, don't be afraid to ask for expenses, for example if it's a shoot for a designer or something of that nature – you might be able to do some work unpaid but if it's costing you money for travel, that is when it can really start to be a problem.

The more established you get, the less you should be doing unpaid work. This particularly becomes an issue when you are being asked to do a job for free when they would usually pay a makeup artist for it. If you're doing a test shoot to build up your portfolio, everyone will be doing the shoot for free in return for images for their portfolio so that's absolutely fine. But if you're doing makeup for a shoot and the pictures are going to be used to promote a certain brand, this is classed as commercial work and you need to be paid. Everyone else on the shoot will be getting a fee, so why shouldn't you? Never be afraid to ask questions.

On that note, I have two stories to share with you. In my first year of trying to work freelance, I saw a post online from a 'director' looking for a makeup artist for an upcoming music video. The post went on to say that it was 'going to be featured on MTV' and would be 'filmed in Swords'. If ever two statements didn't quite fit together they would be those ones. The position was unpaid but would be 'great exposure' and as I was young, totally naive about the industry and full of blind optimism, I emailed him saying I'd love to be involved. He responded, seemed pleasant enough and said that it was confirmed for Monday, which was two days away.

This 'director' had said that the music video was for a rap duo that were originally from Uganda and as I was still building up my kit back then, I knew I didn't have enough foundation shades in my kit for darker skin. With that in mind, and always wanting to be as prepared as possible, I went to MAC Cosmetics, spent €80 on foundations which I couldn't afford (I put them on my credit card) and excitedly prepared to work on something that would actually be on MTV.

The day before the shoot, I texted the 'director', asking him if he could email me the details for the shoot (the location, time, etc.). The response I got was totally unexpected. He basically said that because I asked for the details to be emailed to me I was off the shoot. Presuming I'd misunderstood him or the message was for someone else, I responded asking for clarification. He said that I was off the shoot because I 'asked too many questions'. If I knew then what I know now, I'd see this as an example of someone to be very wary of. If someone doesn't want to give you the details of a shoot, there is something very wrong and you shouldn't get involved. You could be jeopardising your safety as you'll be meeting someone you don't know at a location they won't give you yet. I decided to check out this man's Facebook to see what he'd been up to. He's wasn't living in Ireland any more and didn't seem to have ever had any of his work shown on MTV.

My other story is of a slightly different nature but I think it's important to tell, nonetheless. Just over a year ago, I was working with a news channel that set up a pop-up studio to shoot some features in Dublin to do with an upcoming election. I had to do makeup on the presenter and then six guests in one hour before the show started, so I kept my head down, quickly worked through everyone and then had a chance to just hang back while they were filming.

While I watched, one of the men who worked for the company that was hired to set up the pop-up studio came over to me and asked me if my job was finished. I replied that I would have more touch-ups to do during the ad breaks, but as they were filming, I was done for the moment. He came over very close and said that he thought it was a joke that I got paid for the work that I do. That it was all a scam. He backed me into a corner and suddenly I felt incredibly uncomfortable. His tone wasn't light-hearted; he made me feel small and scared. As the rest of the crew were at the other end of the room filming, they couldn't see what was happening. He walked away like nothing had happened and I was still a bit in shock. I thought, as most victims do, that he didn't really mean it and I just shook it off. Later, when no one was around, he did the same thing but his tone was even more bitter, angry and hateful this time. He stood so close to me and he knew I couldn't get away until he moved out of the way. He had cornered me and was talking quietly, saying, 'It's a joke that you actually get paid for doing this shite', and 'You should be ashamed of yourself and get a real job.' It just went on and on. I froze, not knowing what to do and I felt like I was a kid again, questioning myself. Was it just a scam? Is my job really a joke?

I didn't know what to do. This was only the second time I'd worked with this company and shockingly, I was afraid that if I said something to the lady that booked me, that they wouldn't hire me again.

I never said anything to the company, but haven't worked with them since as they've stopped shooting in Dublin. I think if that happened again, my reaction would be entirely different as I feel much stronger now. I would stand up for myself, tell the woman who booked me the first time it happened instead of letting it continue – no job is worth being made to feel like that. When you're new to the industry, it can be hard to know when you might end up in an unsafe situation. So don't be afraid to ask questions, follow your gut and stand up for yourself when you're being treated badly. Working as a makeup artist is great but you're even greater so never let anyone make you feel like you're anything less than amazing.

5.3 GETTING AN AGENT

An Agent can be a good tool in helping you to grow and expand your business. Agencies can represent everyone from models to photographers, hairstylists and makeup artists and will help to promote you so as to get you more work. In return for this, they take a commission – usually around 20 percent – of your fee. This percentage can increase, depending on which country you are working in. I chased my current agent for three years before she would agree to sign me. I used to set up a meeting with her every six months, bring in my portfolio to her office and ask for her advice on my work. I would write down the main points that she thought could be improved and I'd go home and put them in place. My work kept improving over the years and finally she decided to take me on.

If a client rings an agency looking to book a makeup artist for a shoot, they could either book you specifically by name or they could ask your agent to recommend an artist for their specific type of job. Some artists are better suited to editorial than commercial, or vice versa. If you get booked for a job, your agent will usually email you with all the job details on a callsheet, which usually includes the names and phone numbers of all the crew, the location, start times and anything else specific you need to know. Your agency will also invoice the client for the work you do and chase up outstanding payments so you don't have to. It can take up to 90 days to get paid for a job sometimes depending on the type of company you are working for.

While an agent can be a good thing to have as a makeup artist, it definitely won't solve all of your problems. I remember a few years ago when I set my heart on trying to get an agent, I really thought that all of my troubles would be over if I just had one and that I would get a ton more work. Unfortunately, that wasn't quite the case. While I do get some work through my current agent, 90 percent of the work I do, I've got for myself. As I was an established freelance makeup artist before I signed with the agency, I made an agreement that any work that I could get for myself, I would look after independently. Agents are good to have if you need advice or some help with a particularly difficult client. Agencies are more important for models – it's incredibly rare for a working model not to be represented.

5.4 BRAND SPONSORSHIP, EDITORIAL CREDITS & MAKEUP DISCOUNTS

Brand sponsorships

When an artist is hired by a makeup brand to represent them on photoshoots, at events and at fashion shows, we call this a brand sponsorship. While this can be great experience and increase exposure for you, it's important that you don't jeopardise your integrity for something that might only last a short amount of time. I've always felt very strongly about maintaining my own integrity and could never be sponsored by a makeup brand that I didn't use and love regardless of how much money was being offered. Other artists don't mind this as much, but personally, I just couldn't. I've turned down a number of jobs because they wanted me to sell a product that I didn't like. I care too much about what I do to compromise what I believe and there are some things that money can't buy.

You may be offered little or no money to go on TV to endorse a product but really this only benefits the brand, not you. If you're endorsing a product that is widely known to be of bad quality, people's perceptions of you might change for the worse. If you'd like to work with a specific brand, why not get in touch with them? They'll appreciate you being a genuine fan of the products and you never know where it might go.

Editorial credits

I talked about this in an earlier section. An editorial credit is when you do makeup for a shoot in a magazine and instead of being paid for it, the magazine will ask you to do it for a 'credit': your name at the end of the editorial. It's funny because the rest of the crew will get credited and paid, but hair and makeup usually don't. To make shoots like this worth your while, you can get a makeup brand you like to sponsor you. In return for products for your kit (or, sometimes, payment), you will ask the magazine to credit you along with the brand you've used in the shoot. Say, for instance, MAC Cosmetics sponsor me for a magazine shoot: they will give me ten products, of my choosing, and in return I will get the magazine to credit me as:

'Makeup by Ciara Allen using MAC Cosmetics.'

It's usually the lower-end brands that will want to pay you for a credit, while more luxury brands will let you request some products for your kit instead. Different brands will offer you different amounts of product, with some companies only giving you two products for the credit, which isn't really worth your while. I would also never credit a brand that I don't actually use in my kit.

The catch is that you need to build these relationships with the makeup brands yourself: the magazine won't do that for you. This is where it's good to identify the brands you like, find out who does their PR or who looks after their artist relations in their Head Office. Once you find out who you need to speak to, contact them and introduce yourself. Explain that you do a lot of editorial work and that you were wondering if they would be interested in sponsoring you for your next shoot. It can be difficult to find the right contact but once you do, and they know of you and your work, you're pretty much set up for life. When I get booked for an editorial shoot, I'll email the artist relations department, tell them what the shoot is for and ask if I can credit their brand in return for product. If they say yes, then I can send them a product request-list; if they say no for whatever reason, I will contact a different brand instead.

Some companies are only allowed to sponsor shoots in specific magazines, so don't presume that big brands will sponsor every shoot you do – they won't.

Makeup discounts

It seems crazy that the majority of brands don't offer discounts to makeup artists, because if they love your products, they will recommend them to all of their clients and use them on photoshoots as well as TV, which amounts to a lot of free advertising when you think about it. Off the top of my head I can only think of two or three brands that offer discount programmes for artists. For the ones that do offer discounts, you usually have to apply with proof that you are a working makeup artist and then you will be issued with a membership card that needs to be renewed every year for a small fee. It's really worth doing as it can save you a lot of money on your makeup kit expenses.

STAGE 6:

SETTING UP YOUR OWN BUSINESS, ACCOUNTING & ALL OF THAT BORING STUFF

Without the business it's just a hobby and last time I checked hobbies don't pay the bills

6.1 SETTING UP YOUR OWN BUSINESS

I can't tell you how many times I started writing this section and then through sheer, brain-melting boredom, I shut down my computer, walked away and would literally do anything to make myself feel like I was too busy to talk about accounts. Instead, I would rearrange the fridge, try to draw an angry dog or looked up where and when Tom Hardy was born.

Knowing your finances is crucial. This side of business definitely doesn't usually come easily to us artists, but it's worth figuring it out. If you're on a tight budget, you'll need to figure out how to keep simple accounts: accountants charge around €500 for basic services, but with some help from Google, a bit of time, a lot of coffee and a break every 4 ½ minutes, you might just be able to handle these issues yourself.

The Initial Steps

So, you've decided to setup your own business. I'm proud of you. You're taking the road less travelled and you're ready to get stuck in and give it your all. First things first, you need to decide whether you are going to trade under your own name or a separate business name. I spoke about this in an earlier section and I personally I think it's best to go with your own name, unless you're working from a studio. Again, this is personal preference but I always think it's much easier for potential clients to find you if you're trading under your own name.

Registering your business name can be easily done online for a small fee. Once your business name is secured, you can register with the Tax Office as a sole trader.

Accounts

As a sole trader, you have to take your accounts seriously, because if you don't, you run the risk of getting audited. A tax audit is when a representative of the Tax Office will go through your accounts in great detail, looking to see if there are any discrepancies. The best thing to do is start as you mean to go on: keep things as simple as possible and if you're the only person working in your company, your accounts should be relatively easy to stay on top of.

I do my accounting the old-school way, with a ledger notepad and a pen. You can do all of this on your computer but personally, I prefer paper. You can hire an accountant to do it all for you but as I never felt I had money to spare, I bought an accounting book instead and taught myself the basics. If you own a makeup studio and have a number of employees, an accountant will more than likely be the best option for you but as I'm the only one working in my company, my accounts are relatively easy to do. It took me a good few years to feel comfortable doing my yearly tax return, but now I finally have the hang of it.

Put simply, your accounts need to show your:

- Income: All of the money you've earned.
- Expenses: All of the money you've spent on your business.
- Profit: The number left over when you subtract your expenses from your income.

Income & Expenses

It's important to stay on top of your accounts throughout the year. I usually try to sit down and do them once a month. (Now, in saying that, as I sit here at 1am on a Tuesday morning in June, I still haven't paid my accounts any attention since March – but in my defence, I have been putting all of my time into this book. So selfless, I know). If you do your accounts with a page for each month, you'll keep things organised and easy to follow. Every time a client transfers money into your account, that is your income. If, for example, you get a payment in July, then that income needs to go on your ledger sheet for July.

Your expenses are costs that you need to lay out to keep your business functioning. For makeup artists, this could be everything from buying products for your kit, to putting petrol in your car. It's important to note that you can only put in expenses that you can prove you paid for: this is why you need to keep receipts for everything. If you bought a new foundation for your kit, keep your receipt. If you had to get a taxi to a job, keep the receipt. While there are a lot of things that are deemed business expenses, don't think that you can buy an expensive handbag and claim it as an expense.

6.2 INVOICING & RECEIPTS

An invoice is defined as a document sent to a buyer (or in this case, usually a client) that specifies the amount and cost of products or services provided by a seller. Still with me? Good! In simple terms, say you work on a photoshoot and the agreed rate is €300. In order for you to get paid, you need to send an invoice to that client for €300. It's very important to be very clear about money at all times, because any confusion around it can be very stressful. You need to know before you go on a job how much you're getting paid, who you need to invoice and when your payment will be processed, and whoever booked you for the job should be able to either answer all of the above or point you in the direction of someone that can.

The format and layout of an invoice can be kept very simple and you'll find a wide range of free templates available to download online. Simply download a template you like, edit in your details and then you're all set. Make sure that when you send an invoice, you send a copy in PDF format, which means that it can't be altered. Also give the invoice an appropriate name and number – each year I start my invoices off at number 0001, then 0002, etc.

An invoice needs to include:

- Your name.
- Contact details, including your address, email and phone number.
- Your bank account details, including IBAN and IBEC.
- Invoice date and invoice number.
- Details of the person you are sending the invoice to, including their full name and address.
- Details of the job you are invoicing for, including the job date and the amount due.
- Payment terms (more on that soon).

Here's a sample:

Invoice

From
Your Name
Your Email/Contact
Your Address

For
Client Name
Client Email/Contact
Client Address

Number   Invoice No.
Date   Aug 28, 2017
Terms   30 Days
Due   Sep 27, 2017

Description	Quantity	Price	Amount
Job Description More info on job if needed	1.00	100.00	100.00
Subtotal			€ 100.00
Total			€100.00
Balance Due (EUR)			**€100.00**

Notes
Payment Terms and your bank details (IBAN and IBEC) and other important relative information.

Your payment terms will highlight the date by which your invoice must be paid. Legally a company has 90 days within which to pay you – if they exceed that and the company aren't responding to your emails, you can seek legal advice. Before sending out an invoice, always ask the company what their payment terms are because you need to know whether you're going to be paid in a week or in three months' time so you can plan around it. You can also include your preferred payment terms at the end of your invoice; but know that if the company's policy is 90 days but you specify 30 days on your invoice, you will most likely have to wait for three months anyway.

Make sure to keep a record of all of the invoices you've sent out on an excel sheet like the one below to keep them all organised. This will make your invoices easier to track and you'll know the payment status by filling in the Paid/Unpaid column.

Invoice Record

Date:	Client/Invoice No	Service:	Total:	Paid/Unpaid
Jan.1st	Blossom Media/00001	Full day makeup	€500.00	Unpaid
Jan. 23rd	Hendy Digital/00002	Half day makeup	€350.00	Paid
Feb.14th	Kevin Cat Murphy Ltd./00003	2hr shoot	€200.00	Unpaid
Feb.28th	J.Elliott/00004	Full day commercial	€500.00	Paid
Mar.14th	Fred Allen Media/00005	TV interview	€500.00	Unpaid
Apr. 9th	Aoibh Allen Bride/00006	Wedding package	€650.00	Paid
Apr. 31st	Universal Music/00007	Music Video	€500.00	Paid

PO Numbers

Occasionally a company may ask you to obtain a purchase order (PO) number before you send your invoice. A PO comes from the company's accounting department; it tracks their payments and needs to be put on your invoice. In the last seven years I've only been asked to get a PO number once, but it's good to be aware of them just in case one comes up. Some companies use this process as a way to delay paying you so as soon as the job is over, ask for the relevant contact in their accounting department and get in touch right away. You don't want to give them an excuse not to pay you.

Receipts

A receipt is a written acknowledgement that a person has received money in return for a service. Receipts aren't necessarily required for every makeup appointment, but if a client requests one, you must oblige. I mainly issue receipts for deposits for bridal bookings.

When issuing receipts, be sure to include:

- The amount.
- The date the money was received.
- Who it was from.
- Details on when the remaining balance must be paid (if it was a deposit).
- As with invoices, make sure that any receipt you send out is numbered, in PDF format so it can't be altered by anyone but you, and named it appropriately.

I've included a sample receipt:

Receipt

From	For
Your Name	Client Name
Your Email/Contact	Client Email/Contact
Your Address	Client Address

Number	Invoice No.
Date	Aug 28, 2017
Terms	30 Days
Due	Sep 27, 2017

Description	Quantity	Price	Amount
Job Description More info on job if needed	1.00	100.00	100.00
	Subtotal		€100.00
	Total		€100.00
	Paid (Sep 27, 2017)		€100.00
	Balance Due		**(EUR) €0.00**

Notes
Confirmation of Payment and other important relative information.

Receipts you have received also provide proof of your business expenses. I have a receipt box that I put all of my business receipts into during the month and then organise them when I sit down to do my accounts. When I'm doing my monthly accounts, I sort them all out into stacks for each month. For example, when I'm doing my accounts for September, I'll start at the beginning of the month, record all of my income and then I'll go through my receipts for September, putting the amounts down in the expense column and numbering each individual receipt. Once I have recorded these receipts in my ledger, I put them in a small box for safe keeping should I ever get audited or need to double check something.

6.3 TAX & INSURANCE

Income Tax or VAT?

Which is which? This is a very good question and it was something that confused me for many years. Income tax is tax levied directly on personal income. The amount of tax you will be charged each year will vary depending on how much you earned, how high your expenses were, whether you made a profit or a loss and what your tax credits are. In general, income tax is around 20 percent, but if you are only making a small amount of money in your first few years of business, you will most likely be taxed little to nothing.

VAT is different. For a business to be VAT-registered they must make over €37,500 in a 12-month period. Unless you cracked a market I haven't yet discovered you won't need to worry about VAT for a few years. There are schemes available to help those who are on social welfare to start their own businesses and more information on this can be found from your local welfare office.

You can also open a business bank account if you like, or just keep using your personal one until you're a bit more established. This is completely up to you. To open a business account you will need to have a Company Registration Number.

Yearly Tax Returns

Every year you need to file your taxes by 31 October (or by 18 November if you're filing online). You will always be filing your taxes for the previous calendar year. For example, this October 2017, I will be filing my taxes for 1 January–31 December 2016.

To be able to file your taxes, you will need to know:

- Your total income (the amount of money you earned).
- Your total expenses (the amount of money you spent on your business).
- Your total net profit (the amount left over when you subtract your total expenses from your total income).

Income tax is charged at 20 percent of your net profit (the amount that is left over). If you have tax credits, they will also be deducted from your total net profit and then the final amount left over is what will be assessed when calculating what you need to pay to the Tax Office. You can pay your income tax online by card and a few weeks later you'll get a confirmation that your taxes have been filed for that year. I joke (whilst actually being quite serious) that I'm often surprised that they don't send my tax return back. Back in the days before you could do it online, I would send in my income tax form having inevitably made a few mistakes. I'd have sections crossed out and would feel like a child pretending to do their parents' job. Like, 'Look at me, I'm a grown up, I have car insurance, dentures and know what liability means!' I'm hopefully not jinxing it but, as of 2017, I've never had my form returned asking me if my Mummy would call the Tax Office as children aren't actually allowed to file income tax returns.

Insurance

It's important to consider insurance because if you make a mistake, for example you accidentally give a client a cold sore, she may decide to take legal action. Of course, if you've read the section on hygiene this will never happen, but insurance tends to be relatively inexpensive and can be paid on a yearly basis. You can also make sure your policy covers your kit in cased it ever gets stolen.

STAGE 7:

THE REALLY IMPORTANT STUFF

If I knew then what I know now ...

7.1 MENTAL HEALTH

The following section was very difficult for me to write and it could be difficult for you to read.

I have struggled in my lifetime with anxiety due to an attack I endured as a teenager and I want to share my story so as to help you should you be feeling the same way. If reading about mental health is a trigger please proceed with caution.

It took me exactly 15 years to acknowledge that I was struggling with my mental health. The second my guard was down, I'd be suffocated with fear and didn't know how to make it go away. Having suffered a lot of trauma as a teen, I buried all the things that haunted me deep in the back of my mind. I imagined that all of these bad memories were kept in a purple box with the lid tightly sealed shut. I thought that if I ignored them for long enough, these memories would move on and disappear. I dreamed of the day when I'd no longer have nightmares and see flashes of pain every single time I closed my eyes. I was wrong. You see the more you ignore a problem, the bigger and stronger it gets. Where I used to feel like I was the one in control, this quickly shifted, and my anxiety took the wheel. It affected how I slept, spoke, the way I walked, the sadness in my eyes and the weight I felt on my shoulders every day.

What lived in this purple box was never spoken of until my anxiety became more present in my daily life than I was. I grew up with a sense of fear and a feeling of abandonment that closely followed me through my teens and well into my twenties. This anxiety showed itself in the form of self-harm, a hidden eating disorder, OCD rituals, daily panic attacks, binge-drinking and such deep fear of being alone that I would keep the company of just about anyone. As I'd never spoken of what haunted me, I was stuck. I couldn't move on.

Whenever people talked about going to counselling, I always felt that there was something narcissistic about it. Paying to talk about yourself for an hour a week while someone listened, took notes and asked you questions that had no answer but made you cry. That it was for people who worked too hard, loved too little and had too much disposable income. It was only after speaking to a friend that I realised I had counselling all wrong. You can go and talk about your favourite shade of beige, your need for daily validation because you secretly know you're a horrible person or the trauma that surrounds that extra slice of pizza you ate last month. There's a real healing that comes from speaking openly. If you've gone through something traumatic and have never dealt with it, you mightn't notice, but you carry it with you every day like a parasite or a heavy backpack containing nothing you need. It's a burden that you've become so used to that you no longer even notice it. Being able to talk to someone who isn't in your everyday life, who understands how your brain works and who won't judge you is an incredibly liberating experience.

It took me hitting rock bottom – feeling totally broken down by my anxiety– before I rang a helpline to finally admit to a stranger that I was in a bad way. As I dialled, it was like something outside of myself was slowly pressing each number until I heard it ringing. My instinct was to hang up, but what if they called me back? What would I say then?

Instead, I froze until I heard a voice on the other end that was kind and warm. I was brief, said I was struggling, didn't know where to turn and asked if they could recommend somewhere I could go. Warm tears rolled down my cheeks while I scribbled down the phone number of a counsellor they recommended. She said I should get in touch as she's very nice and works with women just like me every day. I felt reassured that I wasn't the only one with a purple box full of memories. That a life not controlled by my past was possible and my past wouldn't dictate my future.

The funny thing was, as I'd been living with this condition for more than half my life, I became a master at hiding it. No one ever fully knew what I was going through, as I felt at my worst when I was alone. We now see anxiety, in small amounts, as a part of everyday life and yes, it can be, but don't forget that anxiety is a reaction to fear. It doesn't happen for no reason, and anxious people weren't always so. It isn't a personality trait, a funny habit or 'just the way you are', something happened that made you that way. I now see mental health the same way as any other sickness like diabetes, stomach problems or broken limbs: it needs your attention, requires treatment and you need time to recover.

Guilt and shame can ruin your life – they tried very hard to destroy mine. I had thoughts of 'checking out' early but then something crazy happened. Just as I was at the very edge, with the rain on my face, tears falling from my eyes and about to take that final step out into the air, I met Paul. Now, even after 12 years, I still find it hard not to smile whenever I talk about him. We met on Myspace right when we both needed each other. We were going through very different struggles and desperately needed a friend. We spoke online every day for a few months until we decided to meet at a metal gig in Dublin. I can still remember him sitting nervously at the bar with a face full of piercings and a bottle of Budweiser in his hand. He had a shaved head, and was wearing baggy jeans and a black hoodie with a band I'd never heard of on the front. I was there with a few friends, but he came alone so I'd be lying if I didn't say it was a bit awkward at the beginning.

The next day, 10 May 2005 (not that I'm keeping count), we met in Eamonn Doran's, which used to be a great pub in Temple Bar. We stayed there for six hours and talked over a total of four drinks – two each – as money was scarce. That day changed the rest of my life: if our paths hadn't crossed, I wouldn't like to think about where I could've ended up. I'd never had a guy treat me nicely or listen to me when I spoke. I suppose because I never liked or respected myself, people thought they could do the same. I presumed I was worthless because that's how people treated me.

Paul changed my life, and to this day, I still thank him daily. He taught me that I was beautiful and could do anything I put my mind to: like this book. It took a long time for me to take on what he was saying but now, after more than 12 years together, I can't believe how far I've come. I'm now proud of who I am, and had I not gone through all the bad stuff, things might have turned out differently. I now feel like I'm how I was always supposed to be. I still have my struggles, but now I confront them head-on instead of allowing them to build up.

I never thought my life could be this way and if you're struggling, I want you to know that it won't always be like that. We all go through tough times, but they don't last. That's not just a cute phrase from a get-well-soon card with a small kitten on the front; it is the truth. I'm so open with people about my struggles with anxiety because I know every single person has been through something similar. By talking about your issues, it's giving the opportunity for others to feel comfortable doing the same. Sometimes we forget, but at the end of the day, regardless of how much money you have, how many followers you have on social media or what country you were born in, we're all the same. We have the same thoughts, hopes and dreams. We all feel the same pain, joy, sadness and fear. If we can be honest with ourselves about how we're feeling, then we can finally start being honest with each other.

I've always seen makeup as a way of healing. It can make us feel better even on our worst day, is a form of self-expression and can help to give you the confidence to get out there and make things happen. I love to see the transition my clients go through when they're in the chair. It's not just the physical transformation but also their body language. Usually, when they first sit down, they're feeling self-conscious about being seen with no makeup on, apparent flaws and all. It never ceases to amaze me how many women have amazing skin but for some reason are blind to it. As you start applying makeup and distract them with some light conversation, their body language starts to relax. They're now sitting up a bit straighter, are looking you in the eyes when they speak, have slowed down their breathing and have stopped telling you all of the things, in alphabetical order, that they dislike about themselves.

When I'm with a client, I feel responsible for the makeup applied to their skin, but also for how they are feeling about themselves. My job is to help people feel better, not worse. We work in such an intimate space with our clients, and we need to respect that bond. If you have someone who is very anxious, please be kind, don't rush through the appointment adding to their anxiety and help them to relax as much as you can. Treat them kindly.

Mental health difficulties affect us all and the sooner we start paying them the attention they deserve, the better all of our lives will be.

7.2 THINGS I NEED YOU TO KNOW

I have absolutely no regrets in my life, but I do wish that I was told certain things when I was growing up, things that now, aged 30, I fully believe in. So I really want you to pay attention to this part, turn off your phone for a few minutes and read these points very carefully.

Stay away from what is bad for you. This could cover everything from drugs and alcohol to certain types of people. If it doesn't benefit you and your life, then it doesn't really matter.

Life is short; cherish it. Sometimes we forget that we won't be around forever, and neither will our loved ones, so make the most of what you have and enjoy each day.

Don't take anything for granted. In just a few moments, your life as you know it could be turned upside-down and inside-out. Don't wait for something awful to happen to you or to someone you care about before you appreciate how lucky you really are in your life.

Focus on the big picture. Don't stress about the small trivial stuff. In the grand scheme of things, it doesn't matter that you didn't get to put the dishwasher on.

Always cater for a worst-case scenario. I do this for pretty much everything. Prepare for the worst but hope for the best.

Get angry every now and again. By angry, I don't mean violent: that is something very different (that I don't condone). As a woman, I always felt that getting angry was a bad thing, but anger, like every other emotion is necessary sometimes. By repressing one feeling it will only rear its head in another way and that's why depression and anger are so heavily linked. It's funny how differently an angry man is perceived compared to an angry woman. So if you think something deserves your anger and your honest opinion, give it.

Surround yourself with people who make you happy, not miserable. Just because someone is related to you, it doesn't necessarily mean that it's good for you to have them around you.

Be true to who you are. Growing up, I always felt that being different was a weakness, but I got it all wrong. It's one of the best things you can possibly be, so enjoy and be proud of it. Remember difference is a strength, not a weakness.

Do what you want to do and make your own decisions. Don't let anyone bully you into doing things you don't want to and never be afraid to stand up for yourself.

Stand up for yourself. You work far too hard to be messed around, so don't accept it. You deserve so much better than that, even if no one ever told you.

Understand that how you feel and what you think are valid. Just because you feel one way and everyone feels another doesn't make them right and you wrong. Trust that you feel this way for a reason.

Be strong both physically and mentally. This will take some effort so give it some time.

Care for those in need. We all get desensitised to seeing homeless people begging on the street but don't forget that they were born the same as the rest of us. Depending on where they were born and who raised them can drastically change a person's life for the worst. Buying someone a hot cup of tea or just saying hello and acknowledging them means a lot. You never know, if things had worked out differently, it could be you sitting on the ground in the cold with nowhere to go.

Be just a little suspicious and, dare I say it, a bit unimpressed. Don't trust anyone until you have reason to and don't be amazed by things that aren't even slightly amazing.

You are not defined by your gender. Be a strong woman or a sensitive man and don't let society tell you that you should be something different.

Let the past go. It will do you absolutely no favours to keep carrying it around after all of these years so just let it go. Your past will define your future if you let it so please don't give it that kind of power.

Be honest about how you feel. If you're struggling, please open up to someone. Whether you feel it right now or not, you are loved, you are amazing and you will get through this. Being honest is the first step and the moment the words come out of your mouth, you will already feel a little better. Whether it be to your doctor, a counsellor, or a close friend or family member, let them know what's going on and then you can put a plan together for what to do to help you to feel better.

What other people think of you doesn't mean anything. What you think about yourself is much more important.

Know that you are not defined by your weight. At my biggest I was a UK size 20 and weighed 13 stone. Now at my smallest, a UK size 14, I weigh 15 stone: my fat has been replaced with muscle, which weighs more. I look and feel so much better now but if I focused on what the scales told me, I would be very disappointed.

7.3 IMPOSTOR SYNDROME

Do you ever feel like a total fraud? Like you're hiding something? If you do, don't worry, because I do too. My secret is that I have no idea what I'm doing most of the time. Well, I do, but at the same time, I don't. I go on most jobs well-prepared, hoping for the best and praying that no-one will notice that I'm just winging it. It makes no sense, but the longer I work in this industry, the feeling has got worse instead of better. I then watched a documentary about a famous musician and everything made sense. He said that at every concert he plays, just before going out on stage, he's waiting to be caught out. Even though he's been doing it for 30 years and has sold out stadiums all over the world, he, too, feels like a fraud. He added that as soon as he went out on stage and started strumming his guitar, he would forget all about his Impostor Syndrome until the next time. It's good to know that lots of creative people feel the same way I do and that these feelings have a name.

Impostor Syndrome is a concept describing high-achieving individuals who cannot appreciate their accomplishments and instead have a constant fear of being exposed as a 'fraud'. It's nearly a requirement for artists, and I've also dubbed it the 'tortured-artist-syndrome'. You know – when you're just about to create your life's best work, but you're also two brush strokes away from screwing the whole thing up. While it can be difficult to deal with sometimes, I think there is a positive side as it stops you from getting too comfortable, complacent or content which would all lead to your creative demise. Once an artist thinks that they know it all, they have slowly started to die (creatively, not literally). You should always be on your toes, treat every job like the best one you've ever had and never take anything for granted.

If you feel like an impostor, don't worry, perhaps we secretly all do!

7.4 SUPPORT

Creative people can sometimes feel isolated, as we have chosen a different path to the majority of others. We want something more from life and will sacrifice most things to get it. Painters don't get into art because they want to make money. They do it because it's who they are, it's how they see the world, and it's flowing through their veins. The art market is very lucrative, but the artist will usually be dead before their pieces are worth anything at auction. Many painters struggled their entire lives only to die and make an investor a fortune. Art is an investment by those who don't understand or even like it. Art isn't something that is dreamt up in a stuffy office over a team meeting gorging on croissants and cappuccinos. Art is a feeling. It's a vision. A desire for something different. To let others see the world through the painter's eyes. It goes without saying that creatives are a minority in this world and though we're vital for just about everything, from designing album covers to creating advertising campaigns for athletes foot powder, we are, more often than not, misunderstood. We are an enigma of sorts. So if the logical people of this earth see us as strange, shouldn't we be pooling together to support one another?

When I first started out, I thought that I was in direct competition with every other makeup artist in the country. I felt that every job they got booked for, and I didn't, was a point to them and a loss for me. If I saw them out in public, I wouldn't make eye contact for fear that they would see my insecurity by looking at me. It took a few years for me to 'get a clue' and change my way of thinking. I learned that you need to approach every situation in a positive manner instead of in a negative one. Instead of feeling like I was in competition with other artists, I would contact them and compliment them on their work.

Saying that they're good at their job doesn't take anything away from me. Once I started doing this, something unexpected began to happen. These people would tell me that they respected me as an artist and also admired my work. It's like all you need to do is take the first step in the right direction, and then everything else falls into place. Creatives tend to be insecure about their art at the best of times, so if we encourage each other to keep going and not to give up, we all benefit.

Once I started chatting to other artists, I gained many new friends who could recommend amazing new products they'd just discovered and recommend me for jobs that they couldn't do. In essence, being kind and supporting others will, in turn, lead people to do the same for you when you need it. I always say that if creatives don't support each other, what chance do we have?

So here's how we can all help each other:

Be supportive of others

Life is not a competition, and we're not in a race to the finish line. Be happy for others when they do well, and they will hopefully do the same for you.

Be kind to retail staff

Retail is challenging. I think it's the kind of job that should be compulsory so people can understand what sales assistants go through. I did it for about five years, and it shows you another side to the general public. Next time you're paying for your coffee, ask the barista how their day is going. You are then, in my theory, balancing off the last ten people who were rude and you might just make their day a little bit easier. You never know, it could be you making the coffee one day.

Encourage wild ideas

If you have an idea that's a bit out there, like me when I decided to write this book, the worse thing that can happen is that someone has an adverse reaction to it. It can be crushing and could sadly bring the idea to an abrupt halt. When I first told my sister about what I was planning, she replied, 'What would you write a book about?'. She didn't mean to be nasty, it was her instinctive reaction (scarily enough) but don't worry, she's logical, it's not her fault. I called her up on it, and after she had thought about it for a few minutes, she got the message. Her reaction could have resulted in me deleting all traces of this book from my computer and get a job working in a finance company, but luckily it didn't. Surely this is how things get done. How books get written, how movies get made and how clothing lines are dreamed up. It all starts with an idea that needs nurturing, encouragement and as much positivity as you can stuff down its throat. Shutting down someone else's dreams reflects more on you than them. Regardless of how big or small, encourage people to follow their hearts and make their wild ideas a reality.

Listen

We talk over each other in fear of the slightest moment of silence, but it's compelling just to hear someone when they speak.

Be open with people

It took a long time for me to come to a point where I can be open with people about all aspects of my life. Before, I felt I had so much to hide, but now, it feels liberating to speak openly about it. We all need to help and support each other.

7.5 PERSEVERANCE

My level of determination still has the power to surprise me. It's now become second nature to never give up, take no for an answer or stop trying. I do also think that it's one of the most difficult things to do in this industry if you want to get somewhere. When I first went freelance and was trying to build relationships with industry folk, no one ever responded to my emails. It was disheartening. I would always phrase them so nicely, I was friendly and polite but still, my inbox remained empty. I couldn't figure out what I was doing wrong. I was taking the lack of responses personally, but that didn't stop me, and I kept going.

I would periodically follow up on emails (every two weeks) and wouldn't stop until I got a response. People don't necessarily ignore your emails on purpose – they could just be swamped with work, or be out of the country, or both. I mentioned it already, but it is vital that you remain friendly in your follow-up emails. They're not under any obligation to respond to you so sending them an email saying how awful they are for not writing back is not going to do you any favours.

I looked back last year, and for one person, in particular, it took 34 emails over an 18-month period to get a response. I'm not exaggerating that in the slightest. If you read all of those 34 emails, you'd never know how frustrated and angry I was. Instead, when they finally responded, which I knew they would, we set up a meeting, they had a good look through my portfolio, and we've been working together ever since. You can't risk ruining relationships that you may rely on in the future so persevere, don't quit and always be polite.

7.6 HOW TO BE SELF-EMPLOYED & NOT LOSE YOUR MIND

Self-employment can be amazing because you are your own boss, but it can also be a curse for the same reason. You'll never work as hard for anyone else, and as I type these words, it's 2am on a Tuesday morning, so you get the idea. This line of work can have so many ups and downs and highs and lows, but no one ever said that it would be easy. The easy part is when you're with your clients or on a photoshoot, but the hard part is finding the work (or as I like to call it 'the hustle'). Also, doing your accounts is pretty grim, but that's a given.

To give you a giggle, in May 2016 I had a benign tumour removed from my throat, along with half of my thyroid, and I was told I would need ten days to recover. The morning after my surgery, whilst still in hospital, I got an email asking if I was free in three days' time to work with Amy Huberman on a two-day shoot. Without a second's thought I said yes and, three days later, just out of hospital, I showed up on set with limited movement in my neck but with a silk scarf tied in a bow to hide the stitches around my neck. No one guessed a thing. If an opportunity arises, you have to grab it with both hands because they don't happen all of the time. If you have plans but get asked to do a great shoot, know that by saying no to the job you are not only missing out on money for that day but also the client mightn't book you again.

Here are some tips on how to do it the right way:

Understand that you are your business

As you're self-employed, you rely solely on yourself to keep your business going. You can't go into work one day, slack off and hope that no-one notices, because they will. You can't hide in the bathroom because you're hungover when your client is waiting outside the front door of your house. You need to take things seriously and put everything you have, mentally and physically, into your business. If it goes wrong, you're the only one who will suffer, but if it goes well, the rewards are all there for you to enjoy.

No freelance artists have work every single day, so on the days when you have no 'real work', I'd recommend getting up early and make a list of what you'd like to achieve that day. It's so easy to stay in bed late and laze around watching Netflix, but I can guarantee you that around 2pm, you'll start feeling guilty because you really should've replied to those emails, posted those letters and washed your brushes. That guilt can ruin the rest of your day, so don't do it in the first place. If you feel like you can't get anything done, go out for a walk or grab a coffee to get some headspace. You'll come back feeling refreshed and with a new enthusiasm for getting things done.

Don't take it personally

You can easily take things personally when they don't go well, as you are your business. If someone doesn't book you for a shoot or a bridal trial is unsuccessful, it does hurt. Understand that business is business and it isn't a reflection on you as a person. If you always try your best and conduct yourself professionally, that's what counts. Another side of this can be when you're trying to get your work published in a magazine. It can be complicated to get in contact with the right person and, even if they see your work, there's always a chance that they won't like or want to publish it. If you're proud of your work, that's what counts and don't let anyone make you feel any differently about it. If I was proud of an image I created, even if Alex Box and Anna Wintour both thought it was awful, my opinion of it wouldn't change. Opinions are not necessarily based on fact, just a view.

Don't quit

In my first two to three years of self-employment, it was harder than I'd ever expected. I was earning little-to-no money, had a lot of expenses, and it was nearly impossible to make ends meet. I had to sell off a lot of my belongings so I'd have enough money to survive. There were three occasions that I distinctly remember thinking that I would have to quit. It was so upsetting because I'd been trying so hard and didn't feel like I was getting anywhere. It got so bad at one point that I went for an interview for a full-time job in an office, but looking back now, it was a godsend I didn't get it. Through the rough times, I would get upset and let myself be angry, but usually the next day, I would wake up and see things differently. I'd focus on the jobs I'd done instead of those that I hadn't and would have a renewed excitement to keep on trying. So don't quit. You've already come so far.

The bad side

Difficulties can happen in many different ways but try to remember the following:

- Don't trust people until they've earned it.
- If someone promises you something that sounds too good to be true, it might just be.
- If you don't know your worth and put a low value on what you do, people will take advantage.
- Just because someone says something nasty about you, it doesn't mean that it's true. It usually says more about that person's state of mind than yours, so don't take it personally, don't lower yourself to their level and never retaliate. They aren't worth your words or your tears.
- Don't get involved in other people's business.

Try to remember all of those business studies classes you took in school

Because I earned so little in my first few years in business, I learned to survive on a tiny amount of money. Once I had petrol in my car, makeup in my kit and food in my fridge, I was doing great! When you work freelance, you don't get paid a fixed weekly/monthly salary like in other jobs. You could get paid a lot this month but then get nothing for the next two months. You need to learn to put away any money you don't need right now, because unplanned expenses can happen at any time. It could be product restocks or repairs on your car, so try and keep a bit away for when you'll need it. Maintain a record of all your business expenses as well as receipts for everything like petrol and products. Take your business and time seriously, and others will do the same.

Know your finances

It sounds like an obvious one, but people can get uncomfortable when talking about money. I used to be awkward to the point that I would break out in an emotional sweat trying to put together a bridal quote. Instead of quoting a price, sometimes I'd just let them pay me whatever they thought it should cost. I've now learned that I have to think like a business and businesses need income to survive. Be very clear about money and ask when you're going to get paid for a job. Let there be no confusion. If you're running a business, regardless of what that business is, money is vital. If you don't want to talk about money, you're not going to last, I'm afraid. What happens when your rent is due, and you're owed €1,000 but still haven't been paid yet? How do you feel now?

File your taxes on time

As a sole trader you are legally obliged to file your tax return yearly. Keep on top of your accounts throughout the year, and this won't be a total nightmare. A bit of a pain but not a nightmare.

Befriend the self-employed

If all your friends and family are in full-time jobs, chances are they won't understand the highs and lows you'll go through. It's nice to have people around you who know the industry. Being self-employed can be lonely, so don't be afraid to reach out to someone for advice or a chat over coffee. Chances are they might need some help as well.

Don't panic

Work usually goes two ways: you're too busy, or you have nothing going on. No bookings. No calls. No emails. Just tumble weeds. Sure, everyone likes a break every now and again, but this is ridiculous. When you're busy, you fantasise about all the books you'll read, the walks you'll go on and all the coffee you'll drink when you have some time off. But then when work is quiet, you have lots of books, but you just don't quite feel like reading. Instead, you get stressed. You start thinking that you'll never work again and the phone will never ring. You simply can't focus on anything else. Take it from someone who has been there many times: everything will be okay. You will work again. It's not personal; it happens to everyone at some point. Take this time to do some research and contact some potential new clients. Why not organise a test shoot to update your portfolio? Update your website? And if you're bored, your accounts probably need doing.

Stop creeping on social media

Nothing makes you feel worse when you're going through a quiet patch than seeing someone else working on a job you would've loved. Don't get sucked into obsessing what other people are up to; it's none of your business. Your focus needs to be on yourself, not on others.

Find a hobby and volunteer

Chances are you won't have work every single day of the week (although I hope you will). I took up weightlifting a few years ago, and it's helped me through some stressful times. Exercise is a great way to help clear your mind while looking after your health. If you're having a rough day, escape to the gym, turn off your mobile data and listen to some music. Hardcore is my personal preference for the gym. You'll be amazed at how much better you'll feel when you leave. Another great way to fill your free time between jobs is to volunteer with a local charity. There are always organisations crying out for volunteers, so why not give some of your time to those who need it. By helping others, not only are you doing the right thing but it'll also give you a feeling of accomplishment and fulfilment. Putting energy into something positive is so much stronger than putting it into something negative.

Don't doubt

I'm lucky that my husband can double up as my life coach and therapist when I need a bit of encouragement. Things aren't always going to go your way; you won't always be on top and you will go through dark times. Creative people tend to go through periods of self-doubt and insecurity, so we all experience the same thing in different ways. Just know that you're doing great, you're trying your best and you've already achieved so much. Don't forget that.

7.7 THE THINGS YOU'LL NEED TO HEAR WHEN YOU WANT TO QUIT

You can only really understand how hard it is working for yourself when you're doing it. You can read all the books (this one obviously being the most helpful), make business plans in your sleep but until you're in the midst of it, nothing will fully prepare you. You'll go through the highest highs, followed by the lowest lows.

With that in mind, here are some things that might pick you up when you're about to give up:

- Things will always get better. Give it some time, don't make any rash decisions and appreciate everything you've achieved so far.
- Money is necessary, but it isn't everything. Sometimes a job or a client isn't worth it, so don't be afraid to say no.
- Don't feel embarrassed asking another artist for advice. We've all been there, and if they're in any way decent, they'll be happy to help.
- Just because they cancelled you for that job, doesn't mean that they hate you or your work.
- When work is quiet, focus your attention on something completely different. Volunteer, go for a jog, listen to some music and just breathe.
- It's only makeup; we're not saving lives here. Don't worry if you mess up your client's eyeliner. Even on your worst day, it's still a million times better than what she can do on herself, so don't worry.
- Don't be stressing, that's what makeup remover is, for now, isn't it?

- You did what she wanted, down to the last layer of mascara.
- You followed her demands, let her call the shots and if she still doesn't like it, it's nothing to do with you. Forget about it.
- You tried your best. It's not your fault.
- Sometimes a client won't like you, but that's OK. You didn't like her either.

You've come this far; you'd be crazy to give up now.

AFTERWORD

On a final note, I just want to thank you for buying this book, but if you found it on the side of the road, that's also fine. I sent my idea to a handful of book publishers, and no one responded. Instead of me thinking it was because my idea was terrible, inspired by my favourite Henry Rollins, I set-up my own publishing company and took on the task of figuring out how one writes a book. It's been both exhilarating and terrifying at the same time. When you have an idea, and you're investing your own money, there's no guarantee that everything will work out. I've believed so strongly in this idea since day one, as I've done it for the right reasons. It wasn't to make money or to raise my profile. It was because I've learned a lot over the past few years in business, and so many of the things that you need to know are not taught in makeup schools at the moment – and I have a big problem with that. I get emails every week from people asking advice on relatively easy business problems that their tutors never brought up. So here it is. Every ounce of my industry knowledge has been squeezed out, spell-checked and formatted to the best of my ability.

I want to thank you again for buying this book and for supporting someone who has always felt like an underdog in the industry. I've never had anything handed to me in my life or my career, so I appreciate everything and work harder than most. If I can do it, so can you.

Dream big, don't ever take no for a final answer, stand tall and show them what you got!

Love,

Ciara.